# AFRICAN JOURNEY

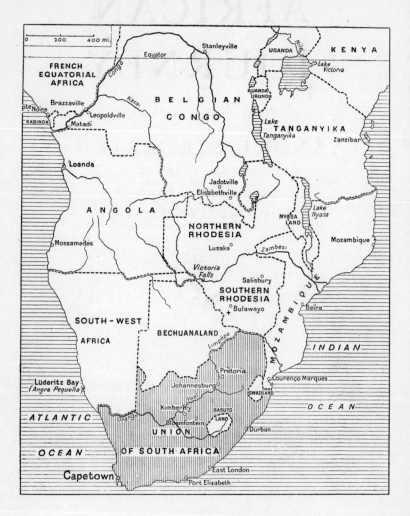

CENTRAL AND SOUTH AFRICA

# AFRICAN JOURNEY

by

ANDRÉ SIEGFRIED

Translated from the French by
EDWARD FITZGERALD

JONATHAN CAPE
THIRTY BEDFORD SQUARE
LONDON

FIRST PUBLISHED 1950

PRINTED IN GREAT BRITAIN IN THE CITY OF OXFORD
AT THE ALDEN PRESS
BOUND BY A. W. BAIN & CO. LTD., LONDON

# CONTENTS

# MAPS

# PREFACE

THESE 'Jottings of a Traveller', which appeared originally in *Le Figaro*, were actually made on the voyage. Noted down from day to day during the course of a four months' journey of investigation to the Belgian Congo, Rhodesia and South Africa, they convey the direct impressions of a traveller, and it is this direct aspect which we wish to preserve by publishing them just as they are rather than giving them the more organized form of a book. In this way reality is brought closer. Each of the following chapters deals with a particular problem which, it is hoped, will prove of general interest.

# CHAPTER I

# THE WHEREFORE OF A VOYAGE

IT seems to me useful to indicate what interest, and in particular what present interest, impelled me to make a voyage to South Africa. It is always fascinating to go and see things in their own surroundings, but the special attraction of this or that particular journey varies from time to time because the zones of high and low pressure in politics shift just as they do in the atmosphere, bringing appropriate changes in the map of world trade routes. It is in this sense that the problems of South Africa call for our attention at the moment: a centre of political depression is in process of forming there.

Two world wars have revealed the insecurity of the Suez Canal route in the event of armed conflict, and thus the route by which Vasco da Gama sailed once again takes on the importance it lost in 1869 and replaces the Mediterranean as the life-line of the British Empire in the new guise it is gradually adopting. This old route, pivoted on that Cape of Storms which Vasco da Gama called 'Cape Hope of India', therefore deserves fresh study. The temperature, sometimes feverish, of the world is reflected in the nature and intensity of its traffic.

The Union of South Africa now occupies a place of first-rate importance in the structure of the British Commonwealth, because the safety of communications between Western Europe and India, Australia and the petrol of the Persian Gulf depend on the Cape route.

The profound significance of the visit made by George VI to this part of the world a few years ago becomes clear from this viewpoint and is seen to have been anything but a mere affair of courtesy or routine. It is, in fact, essential that Great Britain should be able to count on the loyalty of a Dominion thus geographically situated, and it would be fatal for her not to be able to circumnavigate the Cape in an atmosphere of friendship and confidence. The defeat of Marshal Smuts, who is devoted to the well-being of the Empire, and his replacement by Dr. Malan, who is certainly not such an enthusiastic supporter of the Empire, are events whose import for the fate of the British system is evidently much more than merely local. We know from the past with what anxiety Great Britain has always regarded any incident on the route to India. She still does, but that route no longer lies where it did, and today she is keeping an attentive, not to say anxious, eye on the Cape route.

What is this Union of South Africa which thus finds itself placed on one of the key routes of our world? Its political and economic structure demands our attention, and so also does its demographic make-up. We know that it is a double colony composed of two contiguous elements which have never mingled: Boers and British. Which of these two elements is likely to take over the effective direction of the country in the future? Now that South Africa occupies a commanding position the question has become one of primary importance for the whole British world system.

This problem of the rivalry between two sections of the white race rests on another problem, which is more troublesome and fundamentally probably far more grave. There are 2,000,000 Whites in the Union of South Africa, and 8,000,000 coloured people. These latter are at a stage of development which, though immature, is no longer quite primitive, and the possibilities of still further development are indisputable. What place is to be granted to them in a society which derives from our own civilization? If South Africa were what might be called a colony of exploitation, a colony, that is, in which the Whites were masters, and only masters, the solution would be simple, but, to some extent at least, it is a settlement colony, and therefore it includes not only white masters, but also white employees and white workmen. Are coloured workers to be kept out of skilled trades? Are the coloured people to be admitted into the social and political family of a population of which they represent numerically four-fifths?

The same disturbing problem exists in the United States and we know how far it is from being solved there, but at least the U.S. Negroes represent only 13,000,000 out of a total population of 145,000,000. In the Union of South Africa, where the white element represents only a small minority of the total population and where the fecundity of the coloured people is much greater, the ethnic outlook appears fraught with menace. Already a pitiful class of 'Poor Whites' has formed. Sandwiched between the white employer and the coloured forced labourer, with whom they are unable to compete successfully because they possess no technical superiority whatever over him, they are condemned to chronic pauperism. Socially this 'Poor White' cancer is undoubtedly the symptom of an unhealthy state of affairs, and it demands attention, particularly as the country is rapidly becoming industrialized.

The two world wars resulted in very considerable industrial development in the southern hemisphere. Since the second world war it would seem that the British Empire intends to transfer a large part of its production of war materials to its Dominions in the southern hemisphere and to Canada. The Union of South Africa has thus seen its factories multiply. But to what extent is it capable of continuing along this path of industrialization, a path opened for it, incidentally, at the beginning of the century by its own gold mines? There is plenty of capital, largely capital which has fled from Europe. And there are plenty of immigrants, also mostly immigrants who have fled from Europe. But perhaps this double influx, which tends to increase the influence of the British element, is not altogether welcomed by the Boers precisely on that account? This question, like the others we have just raised, quite considerably affects the future of this part of the world.

It is fifty years since I first decided to make this voyage. At that time I was moved by a desire to see and get to know that founder of Empire, the great Cecil Rhodes. I was also curious, though not in the least as a prospector, about the mines, whose 'fabulous metal' was once again intoxicating the speculators and stock-exchange operators of the Old World. I am now about to carry out my old project, but I shall no longer find that amazing statesman and financier there; I shall see only his famous home, de Groote Schur, and his extraordinary tomb in the grand solitude of the Matopo Hills. 'There are places of deep significance for the soul of man,' says Barrès. This is one of them. Morocco is another for our own Lyautey, and they both show us how a man can survive magnificently in his works. But in all its infinite grandeur the work of Cecil Rhodes contains the germs of crisis, a crisis which is all the more important because the destiny of South Africa now intimately concerns the whole of Western civilization.

# CHAPTER II

## ARRIVAL IN THE CONGO

BELGIUM was celebrating with legitimate pride the fiftieth anniversary of the completion of the railway from Matadi to Leopoldville, and in both towns there was a brilliant succession of ceremonies and festivities, quite moving for the few surviving pioneers who could remember a heroic epoch. Having the privilege of being amongst the invited guests I arrived from Antwerp on board the S.S. *Albertville*, and it was through the estuary of the Congo that I entered the colony, the creation of the great Leopold II of Belgium. (See Fig. 1.)

The Congo, the semi-legendary Zaire of the ancients, was discovered by the Portuguese Captain Diego Cão relatively late, in 1482. This bold sea-man, the precursor of Diaz and Vasco da Gama, sailed into the estuary and up river as far as the first rapids, about twenty-three miles from the sea, where an inscription on a rock surmounted by a cross marks the limits of his penetration. Subsequently, during the course of several voyages, he sought to take his vessels still further up the mysterious river, but he found his way barred by a Cyclopaen wall of steep and impassable mountains and boiling rapids.

For three centuries after that the African continent successfully defended itself against the Western intruders, who, although they succeeded in sailing round it, were still unable to surprise its inner secret. The physical formation of Africa resembles an inverted

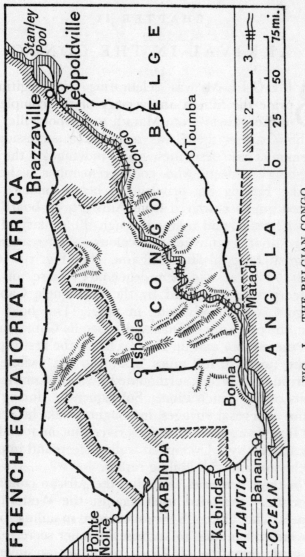

FIG. I.   THE BELGIAN CONGO

plate: an interior plateau descending towards the coast in abrupt gradations bars the way. All the resources of modern technique had to be summoned before the railway line from Matadi to Leopoldville could master a hostile nature in 1898; the line from Pointe-Noire to Brazzaville came much later.

Like all the great rivers of the world, the Congo proclaims its presence in the sea far beyond its estuary. Even beyond sight of the coast the sea takes on a brownish colour and ships seem to be sailing through a kind of syrup. And then, about eight miles wide, the estuary opens up between low-lying mountains, reminiscent somewhat of the mouth of the Scheldt but for the thick jungle along its banks. A dug-out canoe gouged out of a simple trunk of a tree with a native standing upright and paddling, a swarm of a hundred vultures slowly turning in the air — that is Africa. Its fundamental colours are sombre, but a rose-hued tint is met with everywhere here. There are also astonishingly clear and fresh greens, but the crests of the first mountains which can be seen on the horizon are bare and yellow. It is the dry season. It never rains, but perpetual clouds give the general atmosphere a leaden and melancholy tone.

The low-lying plain is very soon shut in by mountains which pile up into an impenetrable barrier. The river, which is navigable by big ships as far as Matadi, just below the first rapids, flows rapidly through narrows that are hardly more than half a mile across. It is at this point that the problem of penetration into the interior first arises, because from here on the Congo is no longer navigable until one reaches Leopoldville, about 220 miles further on where, however, its level is about eighty-five feet higher. Here a magnificent inland waterway to Stanleyville and the Stanley Falls opens up. To solve the problem of its use was to answer the whole question of the development of Africa.

The heroic epoch here was in the last decades of the nineteenth century. It is dominated by four great names: Stanley, Brazza, Leopold II and Thys, the builder of the railway. Involuntarily I was moved by the sight of such historic places, though their history is of such recent date: the pool where Stanley met Brazza, and the Plateau at Vivi where, opposite Matadi, Stanley established his first post for the conquest of the Congo from the west, which he had already mastered in a splendid drive from the east.

Although in his youth he had travelled in Asia, Leopold II never came to Central Africa. It was from his own small European country that this political genius created a new African State, single-handed and without support, with nothing but his own will and determination. The great Belgian historian Henri Pirenne describes him 'standing at the windows of his palace at Ostend and in imagination sailing the seas like another Henry the Navigator'. It was in 1876 that he founded the International African Association, but at that time he envisaged the penetration of Africa from the Indian Ocean.

In August 1877 a sensational event took place: Stanley, the man who six years earlier had found Livingstone on Lake Tanganyika, arrived at Boma at the mouth of the Congo, having crossed Africa from east to west in 999 days.

What he had to tell was a revelation: the Congo-land interior was covered with a splendid network of navigable rivers whose focal point was the Stanley Pool, upstream from the first cataracts in the west. But the explorer himself summed up the situation succinctly: 'Without a railway the Congo is not worth a penny.' And in truth, what was the use of the illimitable riches of the interior if it proved impossible to find an outlet to the sea?

Leopold II immediately grasped the immense significance of the discovery, and when Stanley disembarked at Marseilles two representatives of the king awaited him with a royal invitation to come at once to Brussels. Stanley was an Englishman and he was naturally anxious that his own country should benefit from his discoveries, but at home he met with nothing but coldness and scepticism, so that in 1878 he decided to become the agent of the International Association of the Congo, which Leopold II had just founded, acting, incidentally, not as a sovereign but as a private person. Stanley's instructions, dictated by the king himself, were: 'Build three stations, launch a steamer on the Upper Congo, and maintain communications with the sea.' It was thus that in September 1879 Stanley founded his base at Vivi on the right bank of the river below the cataracts.

From Matadi, which was then nothing but a point of departure, a portage track wound into the interior. I saw that track myself, a narrow path plunging boldly into the steep mountains which sweep away to the horizon. It was along this track that the parts of the river boat destined for the interior river basin were carried, and later it served to carry materials for the first work on the railway line.

In Alaska I saw a similar track, 'the old trail', along which the gold seekers made their way to the Yukon. That was at about the same time, and these heroic memories are hardly more than fifty years old! They are none the less impressive for that.

The very difficulties of this path made it necessary to begin a battle for the railway, which opened in 1887 and was not finally won until 1898. It is that victory which Matadi and Leopoldville, both beflagged and with bunting flying, were celebrating.

# CHAPTER III

# THE BATTLE FOR THE RAILWAY

TH E battle for the railway began in 1887. The Congo Free State, of which Leopold II was king, had been recognized by the Berlin Conference in 1885. Brazzaville was founded in 1884. It was the great period of the opening up of Africa. Cecil Rhodes had already arrived in South Africa.

Without an outlet from the Stanley Pool to the Atlantic the immense riches of the interior were practically useless. A railway was an absolute necessity, but the distance from the Pool to Matadi was 250 miles, and across the most difficult country at that. Captain Thys, aide-de-camp to King Leopold II, was appointed by his royal master to undertake the formidable task of joining up the interior with the sea by rail. It took him twelve years to perform the task, but on March 16th, 1898, the first locomotive reached the Pool and Stanley could telegraph to Thys: 'Belgium can be proud to have built the first railway in Equatorial Africa.'

The work was accomplished by the methods of private enterprise (let us have the courage to call it capitalism), which was still in high honour in the nineteenth century. Leopold II was the powerful spirit, the great patron who gave the orders, but Thys was the prime mover. He was neither an engineer nor a financier, in which he resembled Ferdinand de Lesseps, but he had faith and energy and the determination necessary to bring the grand project which had been placed in his charge to a successful conclusion. Such great captains of industry, who are accused by jealous and malicious tongues of being self-seeking, live in reality only for their work, and although they are practical men above all else, nevertheless we can class them amongst the great idealists who magnified that century of discovery, the nineteenth, which in this respect equalled the fifteenth and sixteenth centuries.

Even today, seated in the comfortable carriage which takes you to Leopoldville, it is easy to imagine the titanic labours which were imposed on those early pioneers. At Matadi there is no flat country at all; not even a natural plain along the banks of the river. The present very fine quays have been won from the Congo itself, whose rapid flow is hemmed in by steep mountains. The town consists of nothing but terraces; all its streets are steep, and motor cars toil up them as though on an alpine railway. The site is splendid but terrible. It is a disorderly conglomeration of mountains, peaks and valleys. It reminds one of a sea lashed to fury, whose immense and erratic waves have suddenly been turned to stone.

It is warm even in the winter of the southern hemisphere. The sun is molten fire, and flowing between its steep banks the Congo is reminiscent of some burning Styx. But it is across those mountains the line must go, rising from gradient to gradient, from ledge to ledge, from valley to valley, until finally it reaches the heights of the plateau. The worst difficulties were encountered in the first thirty-odd miles; once they were overcome, the railway was victorious. After that the country is flat as far as

Thysville and Leopoldville, the ancient Kinshasa, and there are no further difficulties.

From 1900 onwards colonization entered into a new phase, which one might call the scientific period; the heroic era came before that. When Thys began his work in 1887 it was just the time when the conquered Titan, Ferdinand de Lesseps, was tasting the full bitterness of his Panama setback. In those days mechanical processes were still very rudimentary compared with what they were later to become, and hygiene, too, was primitive. It was only ten years later that man began to learn the role played by the mosquito in the spread of the great tropical diseases. The railway line from Brazzaville to Pointe-Noire goes through hardly less difficult country, but it had the advantage of being constructed almost forty years later. Today these two lines, parallel routes, offer a reliable outlet from the basin of the Congo to the sea.

When the line was inaugurated in 1898, with a solemnity reminiscent of the celebrations in connection with its fiftieth anniversary, Pierre Mille was invited to be present as the representative of the French press. That great writer, the poet of French colonization, the Latin Kipling, often described the Stanley Pool to me, and when I finally saw it for myself I found it very similar to his evocative descriptions. It is a sort of inland estuary spread out to a distance of three or four miles and having the aspect of a lake with low embankments. From Leopoldville, on the left bank, one can see Brazzaville on the opposite side. They are two colonial towns which, in the words of Pascal, have their centre everywhere and their circumference nowhere.

At this time of the year the sky is always grey except at sunset, and the result is a certain impression of melancholy. Colours are subdued; the trees are a sombre grey-green, and the muddy shade of the water contrasts with the light green of clumps of verdure carried along by the current. But instead of emerging on the coast this 'estuary' slides almost immediately into a gorge, still very large, in which the flow is broken up by a series of rocks into boiling rapids. The river plunges into seething cataracts, its tossing waves flecked with white foam, and runs on swiftly between steep, raised banks.

A comparison with the immense calm of the Amazon, flowing smoothly between banks bordered by giant forests and navigable by large vessels far up-river to a distance of over 600 miles from the sea, reveals the great difference between South America and this Africa which defends itself obstinately against intrusion, not so much by its forests as by that mountainous barrier which hurls its rivers towards the coast so swiftly that they are no longer manageable. The view, in particular from the Brazzaville ledge, is majestic, immense and, to a European observer, profoundly exotic; nothing we know in Europe prepares us for it.

Leopold II has truly left his mark on the colony which he subsequently presented to his country. At first a private enterprise, it became a State of an entirely new type. The Congo has largely retained this character of a practical enterprise in which three powers, the great financial and industrial groups, the missions and the administration, co-operate to carry out one programme in a pragmatic spirit which is more concerned with results than with empty doctrines. The natives are well treated in a spirit of paternalism which takes account of their still primitive stage of racial development, but which has not as yet squarely faced the problem of ethnic relations which will arise at a later date once the natives have developed to greater maturity by reason of their inevitable contact with the West. The problem is hardly visible at the moment because we are dealing here not with a settlement colony as in South Africa, but with a pure colony of exploitation in which the white man deliberately confines himself to the role of master. The present Belgian colonists, with their efficiency, their awareness of the need for adjustments, and their determination to build a solid edifice to stand firmly on its own feet, have every reason to celebrate the fiftieth anniversary of the building of their railway and do honour to the statues of Leopold II and his servant Thys: their work holds good.

# CHAPTER IV

# THE NATIVE PROBLEM

I RECENTLY made the acquaintance of coloured Africa for the first time and the impressions I record here are naturally devoid of all pretensions. If they prove of any interest it will be chiefly, I think, because of the comparisons they suggest with the colour problem as it exists in the United States. The Negro of the New World is an African, and an African he has remained to this day despite his adaptation to the different conditions of another continent. In the Congo, contact with the white man is comparatively recent, but the two peoples are in fact of the same race. I was immediately struck by certain physical resemblances: their gait, in particular, is the same. At Tuskegee, the university for coloured people in Alabama, I was once a spectator at a football match which was followed by a procession. In Leopoldville and Elizabethville I noticed the same way of walking — a certain forward thrust of the legs, a flowing freedom of movement something like the amble of a horse — and saw the same long, slender legs, narrow hips, broad shoulders and flat bellies.

The women hold themselves especially magnificently. Their habit of carrying every sort of burden on their heads, makes them look like graceful and dignified caryatides. When they walk their arms are held slightly to the fore as though to balance their burdens. The runners in a 400 metre race at the Leopoldville

Stadium were an excellent example of what the human body can offer in the way of energy, suppleness and speed.

At work — and this is the experience of all the employers of labour I consulted — the coloured labourer unquestionably reveals technical ability. It is easy to teach him a trade and he will usually become very skilled at it, providing always that nothing is expected of him beyond a certain level. It is this level which marks the real borderline between the primitive native and the civilized White.

The native is not quick, but he is capable. He grasps what is explained to him provided the explanation is concrete and practical and he is then made to repeat what he has learned. One must not demand initiative from him or reasoning, but only application and memory. That is the limit of his capacities. But then, and with that qualification, his limitations turn to advantages in production. As long as his imagination is not called upon he will not complain that work is dull or tedious. His patience is infinite and he can be more careful than the white man, particularly as his senses, younger and nearer to nature, have remained more acute. Through the microscope for instance he can see details which escape our European eyes.

In these circumstances and under proper guidance he is a useful and efficient workman: certain trades which represent a continuation of an old artisan tradition are particularly suited to his talents, and I have been told the same thing in the United States: for instance, he makes a good moulder and a good carpenter. And when it is a question of art or rhythm he

26

reaches an even higher level of skill. In textile mills the designing is left to him and he demonstrates an inventiveness and a fantasy and a sense for colours and harmony which the European worker does not normally possess to the same extent.

These observations apply only to the men. The women are less developed, and generally speaking they have proved unsuitable for work in the factories. It was hoped to employ them usefully as textile workers, but experience soon showed that they are unable to adapt themselves to machinery. They have been seen dancing to the periodic and regular rhythm of a trans-mission belt. The inferiority of the coloured people is not individual, but social and collective, a point we shall return to later on.

In the Belgian Congo the coloured workman has had no difficulty in learning to do skilled work; and, unlike his counterpart in South Africa, he has been systematically encouraged to do so, for here we are dealing with a colony of exploitation in which the European plays only the role of master. The dividing line fixes itself because, as has been said, when questions of reasoning, adaptation and organization arise, the limitations of the native are revealed. He can use his memory, grasp ideas and accumulate experience, but that is all. Sometimes it has proved possible to employ natives as foremen, but that is still the exception. With work which goes on automatically and without difficulty once it has been started the native workman can be left to himself, but at the least breakdown necessitating repairs or re-organiza-tion the white man must intervene again.

From this the believer in white racial superiority in

South Africa and the United States draws the conclusion that the inferiority of the coloured people is congenital and permanent. Experience, however, suggests a different conclusion. For instance, when he lives in a Western environment the coloured man is quite capable of raising himself as an individual, but collectively, racially, his progress is much slower, and up to the present it has manifestly not been sufficient to place him on a level with the race which, in comparison, can still be described as superior. What he lacks is not so much the ability to develop himself as an individual, as that slow cumulative acquisition of values which centuries of civilization have given to us.

Our indisputable superiority is based less on our technique properly so called, which can be copied, than on a now quasi-hereditary use of scientific methods which have developed into collective practices in our hands.

Its basis is our mastery, which has really become general, of Greek reasoning as perfected by such leaders of thought as Bacon and Descartes. The Babylonians were remarkable surveyors, but only the Greeks were geometricians. This same fundamental difference still exists between the white and coloured races; the former, to use a striking expression of Peguy, know how 'to conduct their thought deliberately as though it were an action'.

It would seem that the coloured peoples are capable of raising themselves, even that they must raise themselves, but it is a question of time, so to speak a process of maturing. An attempt to prevent their rise arbitrarily, such as is being made in the United States and in the Transvaal, involves the danger of a revolt like that of Spartacus in the days of old; and any attempt to accelerate it excessively will invoke the same peril. We all know that technique can be acquired more easily than culture. Now the Negro, artist that he is, is racially still a child. That is quite charming when it is a question of play or even of sentiment, but it can be terribly dangerous if the child should think himself a man and try to play the man. He then reveals all the faults of the *nouveau riche*, his vanity, his pretensions and his inability to take his own measure. The simplest 'clerk', as they say here, imagines himself the equal of the highly educated, and the most obscure petty lawyer feels himself called upon to be a leader of men. Fundamentally the race is mystical and there is thus a danger that the 'prophet' may flourish. We should then find ourselves faced with religious leaders whose emotionalism might easily turn to xenophobia.

Not long ago Matadi experienced a prophet who might well have been born in the United States, for in the United States I could claim that I was Elias resurrected and there is nothing to suggest that I should not find many people, both white and coloured, to believe me. And in Africa, even more than in America, such things can lead to uncontrollable and highly dangerous explosions.

The coloured problem seems primarily a matter of development. The particular degree of development can obviously not be the same in New York or the Antilles, where the contact of the coloured man with white civilization goes back several centuries, as in the Belgian Congo (of which I am exclusively speaking here), where such contact has existed for little more than a generation. The less developed the native, the easier the solution of the problem. When the race regarded as inferior accepts its inferiority and does not even dream of disputing it, the White naturally finds this agreeable, and, in fact, the coloured man then becomes a sort of familiar and affectionate younger brother whose presence is welcome, and the habit develops, all too easily, of calling on him to serve and assist in everything which requires a little effort. But when that young associate, who is loved like a sort of friendly dog, aspires to raise himself to the level of the White, and wants to do it more quickly than is agreeable to the latter, then a crisis arises, sudden and terrible, and affection can then change abruptly to hate.

There are some parents who can never get used to the idea that their children must grow up, and who continue to treat them as though they were still ten years old when they are, in fact, already adult. But it is impossible to prevent children growing up. The right measure in the treatment of another race is a political problem of the greatest delicacy. The native in the Congo is racially still young and therefore the problem of his colour hardly arises, and the paternalist solution adopted by the Belgians is still well suited to the existing circumstances.

In the United States, in South Africa, and elsewhere too, the question can become virulent.

# CHAPTER V

# THE BELGIAN CONGO

JUST as one cannot hope to understand Morocco
without Lyautey, so it is impossible to conceive
of the Belgian Congo without Leopold II. This
great king of a small country created an immense
colony, so to speak, from scratch. At first it was an
independent State under his own personal sovereignty,
and ever since it has retained to some extent the
characteristics of a State. France has unquestionably
placed her mark on Morocco, and Belgian influence is
equally unmistakable in the Congo.

The genius of Leopold II was authentically that of a
great man of affairs of the nineteenth century, a
conqueror, a builder and, in the last resort, an idealist
ready to sacrifice his personal fortune to his great
project. The Belgian Congo still bears the marks of its
origin, and even today it creates the impression of a
splendid enterprise most efficiently managed.

To the French the Belgians with their vivacity,
their caustic humour and their ingenuity in circum-
venting the letter of the law, seem something like
brothers, but in some respects perhaps they are more
like the English, particularly in their business sense,
their objectivity and their possession of a practical
spirit emancipated from the vain slavery of principles.
From this point of view Belgian colonial works have
an affinity with those of England, and one cannot
deny that they have been successful.

Despite a high level of technical achievement magnificently up to date, we seem to breathe something of the atmosphere of the nineteenth century in Brussels even today, and the Belgian Congo creates the same impression; the capitalist age with all its efficiency and its firm conviction that it is serving the cause of progress, still exists. Under a strong and enlightened administration the Belgian Congo is still a colony of business affairs, big business affairs. Leopold II desired it so, and the Belgian Government, even when it is composed of Socialists (the modern form of Conservatism), has kept up the tradition. Its aim is to be successful, and one gets the impression that the administration, the big undertakings and the Christian Missions all collaborate spontaneously to the same end. That amounts to saying that the whole conception is aristocratic, if by aristocratic we mean an administration in the hands of capable leaders.

As it is a colony of exploitation where the white man deliberately confines himself to the role of leader, the problem is relatively simple. There is no question of colonizing territory, whose climate is almost wholly equatorial and tropical, with Europeans, but of exploiting its latent resources. The White need not work there as he works at home; he makes the native work under his direction. But the native himself is still very close to nature, and the country is terribly sparsely populated. Now although this makes the economic problem difficult, the ethnic or social problem is relatively easy, because the native, only at the very beginning of his development towards our civilization, does not at present feel the slightest aspiration towards independence.

The natural resources of the country, both mineral

and agricultural, are very considerable, but the native population is hardly more than 12,000,000, whilst the Whites number only 36,000 of whom 24,000 are Belgians (1947 Census). Thus labour power has to be employed economically and utilized to the full.

In a spirit of paternalism, and under the direction of powerful undertakings well provided with capital, everything is being done to give the coloured population a technical training, and no obstacles are placed in the way of their advance. There is no 'colour bar' here as in South Africa to exclude the native from skilled trades where he might compete with the white worker. On the contrary, a systematic effort is being made to train the natives into skilled workers, and at every new stage of the process the role of the White is more and more circumscribed to that of master, which is, in fact, the intention. Thus the White is predestined to superiority to the extent to which the native progressively raises his own level. In the same way, where the tillage of the soil is concerned the native is left to perform the simpler work requiring no very special technique, whilst the White on the other hand naturally turns towards such work as requires science and skill, and here he plays only a directing role. This attitude of the authorities naturally limits the number of Europeans the colony is capable of absorbing. Only highly skilled and competent men are admitted; all others are systematically eliminated.

Mechanical aids are used to the utmost, because even the supply of native labour power is very limited. The continent, in fact, is acutely short of man-power. The slave trade of former days, chronic under nourishment and sleeping sickness have largely denuded the land of its inhabitants. The first task is to rebuild the population, to see that it is well fed in order to make it efficient, to preserve the gains by an appropriate system of hygiene, and to give the natives the will to exert themselves.

Thus the social aspect is decisive in the whole attempt to utilize the resources of the colony. The Christian Missions were the first to realize this but the mining and industrial enterprises soon adopted the same view, not merely as a duty, but as a matter of clearly understood self-interest, and, finally, as a necessity. In consequence even the lowest wage rates are increased by all the indirect social services they include. There is no jealousy towards the native worker, who is not a competitor, and thus no intermediate class of 'Poor Whites' can possibly form here, as it does almost inevitably in settlement colonies where coloured workers and Whites are both recruited to perform the same tasks in factories and workshops.

There can be no competition between the coloured people and the Whites in the Congo until the coloured worker raises himself to the directorial level, something which lies very far in the future and is practically inconceivable at present because the Congo native was amongst the very last to come into contact with civilization. This is the root cause of that impression of social and ethnic peace which prevails in this colony, where the White does not defend himself aggressively against the coloured worker as he does in the Transvaal. There is no talk to the coloured man about political rights, but only about social and material progress and a better standard of living.

A solution which ignores ideologies is appropriate to the present stage of development of a race which is as yet still inferior — provided that it lasts, for pretensions outdistance progress; today the world hardly has any water-tight compartments left.

Belgium hesitated to accept the magnificent gift offered to her by the sovereign of the Congo Free State. Today it is easy to see to what extent she is entitled to congratulate herself on the possession of such an immense territory. The rapid post-war recovery of Belgian economy was due to the fact that in 1944-45 Antwerp was the only continental port at the disposal of the Allied Powers and also to the fact that war-time devastation on Belgian territory was relatively limited, but we must also remember— not to mention the intelligence of the interests involved — that the Congo as an exporter of copper, tin, diamonds, palm oil and rubber has provided Belgium with a constant flow of those precious dollars of which the rest of the world is so short.

In this respect the role played by the Congo during the war was of fundamental importance. It remains so today and it will continue to be so tomorrow if some new world conflict breaks out. Our European countries, limited in territorial extent, have need of such overseas dependencies which can serve as places of refuge if need be. From this point of view the Congo functions as a State, not as an independent State, but one capable of industrial autonomy, because its isolation from its parent country has turned its development in the direction of industrialization. The doctrine of the Colonial Pact, according to which colonies should not industrialize themselves, is henceforth out of date. Factories are being built everywhere around Leopoldville, Elizabethville and Jadotville.

And finally let us recall that the Belgian Congo (like the French Congo incidentally) is situated on the trans-African route, whose importance in the event of war has already proved itself fundamental. If the Suez Canal route should prove unusable there is only the sea route round the Cape, and that is very long.

In such circumstances therefore the overland route from the Atlantic to the Sudan, Egypt and the Indian Ocean would become of first-class military importance. The two railways, from Matadi to Leopoldville and from Pointe-Noire to Brazzaville, would appear to be the key to the system, for they permit access to the interior of the Congo. Intercontinental routes and world centres of gravity change with the years. This region is well on the way to becoming one of those which count in the struggle for world mastery.

# CHAPTER VI

# JOHANNESBURG

THE Veldt, the Boer Commandos, Kruger and Botha, Cecil Rhodes and Dr. Jameson, in my youth these famous names, since become legendary, filled the columns of the press day after day. It all came under the heading of what the American press succinctly terms 'News', that is to say it was sensational, warlike and charged with heroism, reflecting in a thousand facets the lure of 'the fabulous metal' that has so stirred the imagination of men. All my life with intense curiosity I have tried to picture those elevated plateaux through which the Dutch farmers of the Cape trekked, fleeing before the advance of an aggressive civilization pressing hard on their heels, and that great mining area, the Rand, ripped open and turned inside out by the seekers for gold and subsequently exploited and systematically organized by large-scale capitalism, the most powerful, the most authentic and the most classic of any in the nineteenth century. Shall I confess that coming upon this country from the sky, a country so young and yet already charged with history, it seemed to me more beautiful, more picturesque and more magnificent than I had ever imagined?

The first impression on coming from the equator into the southern winter, which is the dry season, was the change in climate. The sky of the Congo, always grey in an atmosphere heavy with heat which never resolves into rain, is oppressive; its pallid tones are funereal despite the richness and luxuriance of nature spread out below. When one catches a glimpse of the ground below, bordered here by the virgin forests of equatorial Africa, it rolls away interminably in sombre browns and greens subdued in tone, endless plains with relatively sparse woods and clearings. And when the blue sky appears again at Katanga it is still above the same immensity of nameless territory which appears practically denuded of life. Rhodesia, too, offers few landmarks to the view: the Zambesi, a powerful river which seems to wind its way slowly and with difficulty through a chain of mountains; the Limpopo, whose blue and sinuous flow loses itself in the far distance; a few exotic mountainous chains in the form of imperious barriers with rocks jutting up like violet mounds from amidst forests whose trees resemble frizzy heads. . . .

But when one arrives in the Transvaal it is the great expanse clear of all vegetation which is so striking, the immense extent of the plateau limited only in the far distance by the violet outlines of bare mountains. The atmosphere has changed.

It is no longer that of an equatorial country, but, at a latitude still tropical and corresponding to that of southern Brazil, it is, thanks to the altitude (Johannesburg is 5500 feet above sea level), that of the temperate zone. The purity of the air, the crystalline clarity of the horizon, the exquisite delicacy of the distant view recall similar regions to the mind: New Mexico, Arizona, the Canadian prairie at the Rockies, Algeria at the approaches to the Sahara. . . .

It is at night especially that one perceives that geographically one is very far from home. The

Southern Cross is high in the sky and towards the north the Great Bear has almost disappeared, leaving only the beam of the Plough still visible, upright as the bowsprit of some vessel sinking backwards vertically into the sea. I cannot say, even spurring myself into a literary mood, that 'the fiery Southern Cross (quite modest in reality) bursts upon the eye', but nevertheless it is this disappearance of the constellations which are so familiar over our northern latitudes which primarily emphasizes for me the fact that I am so far from home.

The scenery emphasizes our distance from our normal surroundings. On these great plains denuded of vegetation the rare farms surrounded by eucalyptus trees are the only landmarks. The ground, green in winter, is brown, almost ochreous, at this season. The colouring is that of the steppes with a southern tone which is distinctly exotic. Spain has similar areas, and perhaps one might recall our own Causses de l'Aveyron with its yellows and greens in a minor key. It is quite clear that neither the peopling of this country nor its cultural conditions bears any relation to European standards. It is a country of colonization, originally uninhabited, in which both Whites and coloured people are really newcomers.

But the presence of gold suggests other analogies, for it has revolutionized the country, even its appearance. When the plane lands near Johannesburg and the car subsequently takes you into the town it is clearly a mining city marked by all the characteristics of the mining industry in its heroic age. There are innumerable dumps and miners' quarters even within the limits of the capital itself. But take care, the resemblance is not to our mining towns in Europe, but more to Broken Hill in Australia, a mining centre in the middle of a desert. The reason for this lies largely in the nature of the tips, which are clear-cut, geometric mountains, capped cones, some of them of a remarkable chemical yellow and others so white and snowlike that glimpsing them through the mist of smoke and fumes which rises from the ground one might almost think one were looking at the summit of some glacier. And the mining quarters to be seen on all sides are inhabited by coloured workers living in rows of tiny uniform houses like the cells of a honeycomb.

The surroundings lack plan, and it is not difficult to realize that the town has grown up around the mines. A few minutes drive in the car and you find a succession of streets whose aggressive architecture reminds you of America. It is not some rural Main Street they resemble however, but Broadway rather, perhaps the Broadway of twenty or thirty years ago. It is an Anglo-Saxon world, semi-American, semi-colonial: a business centre with streets laid out in chess-board pattern, and all around is a great diversity of suburbs, whose fine villas are surrounded by gardens with semi-tropical vegetation: jacaranda, mimosa, eucalyptus and magnificent willows. One feels that riches sprang up here suddenly; people are avid for luxury and no attempt is made to hide or tone it down as is the case with us. The mining area of the Rand is crossed by rocky barriers which enclose the town so that the surroundings are not like a plain, but irregular like the lands around Nîmes. A walk through Johannesburg is a constantly varying experience; sometimes the impression is of a factory in full blast, sometimes of a street lifted direct from Chicago or Detroit, then of a shady park with southern villas, and then of an exotic labouring city where dark skins predominate.

In turn it is sordid, luxurious and businesslike. In one place it is as bustling as a stock exchange in a boom; in another, as restful and charming as a country club. And all the time above your head there is a limpid sky, unbelievably blue, and around you a tenuous, bracing, almost rarified air, suggesting that the virgin wilderness, which makes this town the capital of a young country, is very close. One must always remember that this town of Johannesburg is hardly sixty years old. Before the decade 1880-90 there was nothing on its site. The sudden, torrential influx of gold prospectors, speculators, financiers, of capital, machinery and a whole army of labour, always in insatiable demand, has revolutionized the atmosphere. Development is rapid, but the past still remains close at hand. It strikes me as impossible to understand the situation here unless we consent to regard it as still existing in the nineteenth century, the heroic age of untrammelled and creative capitalism. This young town, hungry for technical progress, nevertheless retains more than one trait of old England, and Victorian England at that. But this sudden upsurge, reminiscent of a wild-cat oil gusher, has produced more problems than it is able to solve.

# CHAPTER VII

# AFRIKANDER AND
# FRENCH CANADIANS

IF we leave aside for the moment the question of colour and consider only the rivalry between the British and the Boers (or rather Afrikander as they call themselves) we shall think instinctively of French Canada because there we meet with a similar situation. Let us make the comparison, because it throws a new light on the South African problem.

The British Commonwealth includes various kinds of Dominion, that is to say one-time settlement colonies which first became autonomous and then independent within the bosom of the Empire and united under one king. The idea works perfectly well when it is a question, as in the case of Australia and New Zealand, of homogeneous Anglo-Saxon societies derived from England. It also works fairly well when it is a question of Anglo-Saxon societies containing foreign minorities within them and united to them by conquest, as in the case of Canada. But it works only indifferently well when it is a question of societies of the white race, speaking English certainly, but joined by conquest or force to the British Empire, as in the case of Ireland. Then there are such Dominions as the two Indias, Hindustan and Pakistan, which are not even of the white race, and in respect of which, it seems to me, the term Dominion is not properly applicable at all.

How shall we classify South Africa? In one sense

with Canada, and in another with Ireland. Let us see why.

The Union of South Africa has 2,373,000 white inhabitants of whom approximately 60 per cent are Afrikander of Dutch extraction speaking a tongue, Afrikaans or Taal, which is derived from Dutch. They are the Boers of the Transvaal and the Orange Free State and the former Afrikander (though the term is no long used) of Cape Colony. As we know, the Boers retreated before the advance of Western civilization which was pressing on their heels, and in the great trek of the first half of the nineteenth century they sought their liberty in the immense spaces of the upland plateaux of the Orange Free State and the Transvaal. Unfortunately for them, gold was discovered in their new country, and before long they were joined by a cosmopolitan population, chiefly English, which claimed sovereignty there too. After heroic resistance the two Boer Republics were defeated and their territory annexed. That was exactly fifty years ago and many of us can still remember it all. And the Boers remember it too. Apart from the fact that the Treaty of Paris was concluded in 1763 the history of the French Canadians is no different.

In the one country as in the other the conqueror showed himself generous — for he was English — or, if you prefer, liberal and wise. The vanquished, both French Canadians and Afrikander, were granted the same political rights as their conquerors. Under the Dominion regime the French citizen of Quebec and the Afrikander of Pretoria are both electors, and in the usual parliamentary tradition they can make and unmake ministeries to the extent to which they succeed in obtaining a majority. The Governor-General, who represents the King, is appointed by the latter at the recommendation of the local government, which is itself responsible to an elected parliament. Officially British influence properly so-called is exercised only through the intermediary of a High Commissioner, who carries out approximately the functions of an ambassador of the old country to the former colony, which is no longer a colony at all except in its origin. The vanquished in their turn have regained their independence. But what is their attitude towards the British?

I see three differences between the position of the French Canadian and that of the Afrikander. French Canadians are in a minority and represent only about 30 per cent of the total population of Canada, whereas the Afrikander are in a majority and represent about three-fifths of the total population of South Africa. Then the French Canadians are Catholics whilst their fellow citizens are Protestants, whereas the Afrikander uphold the reformed religion, and whilst they are opposed to the Anglicans the difference between the two denominations, real though it is, is not so great as is the case in Canada. And finally, the conquest of Canada lies a couple of hundred years back whereas in South Africa it is still very recent. Many people are still living who took part in the fighting, who saw their homesteads burned down, and who suffered in concentration camps. The memory is not dead, it lives on. To a certain extent it is kept alive by monuments and the celebration of anniversaries, which the British in their liberalism do nothing to prevent.

But after taking these things into account, the position of the French Canadian and that of the Afrikander are curiously similar and one helps to explain the other. In both countries the vanquished have preserved their own tongue, and it enjoys official recognition. They are free to practise their own religion; they have freedom of speech, and full freedom of political action. Nothing in their status makes them in any way inferior to the British. Perhaps the conquerors still adopt an attitude of superiority which is wounding, but that is only from a social angle, and one might well ask what more, apart from complete independence, either the French Canadians or the Afrikander can still obtain politically.

Realizing this situation a certain number of French Canadians and Afrikander have embraced the English regime cordially and with deep sincerity. Men like Laurier, Botha and Smuts have become the Prime Ministers of their Dominion; what is more, they have become devoted collaborators in the British system. 'I am British to the core,' declared Laurier, and during the two world wars Smuts devoted himself wholeheartedly to the British cause. I have just deliberately used a term which has taken on a special significance since 1940, and there is more than one French Canadian in the province of Quebec and more than one Boer on the Veldt who thinks that these two great ministers did, after all, 'collaborate' in that sense. They did, in fact, recognize the regime of the conqueror.

Others, at the bottom of their hearts, have not done so. I believe that, if it were at all possible, many citizens of Quebec would wish for a French Canadian

Republic independent of British Canada and perhaps even independent of the British crown. It is probable that the majority of Afrikander, who were once republicans, would desire a South African Republic, either completely independent of Great Britain or attached to the Commonwealth by ties as loose as those which now bind the Republic of Eire.

There are various different standpoints here. Although the Afrikander of the United Party led by Field Marshal Smuts accept the British regime in good faith, amongst the members of the Nationalist Party, which recently defeated the United Party at the polls there are many — perhaps a majority — who, in their hearts, are separatists. This does not mean that their leaders, who bear the responsibilities of power, intend to press for separation, or even desire it. They can agree, as the Herzog Ministry did before them, to remain within the Commonwealth. But we can imagine what their attitude would be, in the event of war, because we know what the attitude of French Canadians would certainly be if they were, like the Afrikander, in a majority. When Great Britain went to war the French Canadian declared: 'It's England's war and none of my business.' There is no doubt that the Afrikander would say the same thing, and we know, in fact, that it was just on this question that Herzog broke with Smuts with the result that only a very narrow parliamentary majority pronounced itself in favour of entering the war. Perhaps the fact that a war now would be an anti-communist one would alter the case, but it is still questionable.

Canada has only a minority of French Canadians, and although they make their influence felt it is not they who direct Canada's policy. But being in the majority the Afrikander, if they were all of one mind, could direct their country's policy with as much freedom as though they were completely independent. If they cannot do so at present it is precisely because they are not of one mind. The British are in a minority, but as against that they dominate the country's business affairs. The Jews, who are very powerful in South Africa, conform with the British because, naturally, they look askance at certain tendencies of the Afrikander which are more or less inspired by Hitlerism and the Ku-Klux-Klan. Many Boers, who are members of the United Party or the Labour Party, feel quite at home under the British regime, which fully respects the autonomy, let us even say independence, of the Union of South Africa.

There is no separatism amongst French Canadians, or if there is then it is so deep down in their hearts that it hardly counts at all. In fact there is probably more amongst certain pro-American Canadians of British stock. The visible separatism which exists in South Africa amongst the Afrikander remains potentially active because the grudge against the former conqueror has survived down to this day even amongst the younger generations. Need we be astonished at this if we remember that the Southern States of the Union are still far from having forgiven the Northern States in the matter of the civil war?

The British Commonwealth is supple enough both in its structure and in its spirit to devise a type of association fitted to accommodate this attitude of the Afrikander. We shall return to this question later when we examine the relations between the Union of

South Africa and the Commonwealth. However, it seems to me that it is along the lines of the Eire solution that we must look for an example likely to throw light on the problem. Anglo-Irish relations, even in their latest form, are not entirely bad.

# CHAPTER VIII

# AUSTRALIA AND SOUTH AFRICA: THE COLOUR PROBLEM IN THE TRANSVAAL (I)

AS Duhamel has so aptly remarked, South Africa is a land of problems: the colour problem, the Anglo-Boer rivalry, the revolutionary transformation of an agricultural society by gold mining, and by a rapid process of industrialization hurried on in particular by two world wars. These problems are complicated by the fact that the Union of South Africa consists of two former British colonies, Natal and Cape Colony (the latter formerly a Dutch colony), and two former Boer Republics (Transvaal and the Orange Free State). I propose to record here my first impressions of the Transvaal, which I saw early in my journey.

Four chief impressions result for me from a first view of the country. In order to understand its social problems we must go back more than a hundred years to the days when the industrial revolution created a proletariat in Europe which was at first unable to organize itself or to defend its interests. The air one breathes here is that of the nineteenth century with all its social harshness, but at the same time with all the possibilities of its liberal capitalism. This country, young as it is, cannot be understood except in terms of the past. If one bears in mind that the proletariat in South Africa is a coloured proletariat one realizes at once the gravity of the problem, because here a social problem is aggravated by an ethnic one. Its gravity becomes still more disturbing when we take a look at the population figures (1946) and discover that the 2,373,000 Whites form a percentage of only 20.8 out of a total population of 11,392,000, whilst there are 7,805,000 Negroes, or 68.5 per cent, 928,000 Mulattos, or 8.1 per cent, and 285,000 Indians, or 2.6 per cent. The white race thus represents only a small minority, and white people in South Africa are beginning to ask themselves, almost with fear, whether they will be able to survive, and whether in fifty or a hundred years time the country will still belong to them. This instinctive pessimism colours all the judgments of South Africans. Young countries are the countries of the future, but in this country the Whites are asking themselves whether, in fact, the future here belongs to them at all.

A parallel case, which will permit us to regard the problem from one of its most essential angles, came to my mind at once; that of Australia. Here are two British settlement colonies which both found themselves faced with the colour problem, but which have solved it, or set out to solve it, in different ways. Australia has systematically excluded from her territories everything which is not authentically White, but South Africa, which, to tell the truth, has not had the choice, is a country with a coloured working population. We find the same contrast between the Northern and Southern States in the U.S.A., and we know that in this case the result was civil war. At this point the question quite naturally arises: which is better off, Australia or South Africa? Is it better to have a coloured labour army or to dispense with its services in order to obviate an ethnic problem? The answer has a social and an economic aspect.

Australia is a continent sparsely populated by about 8,000,000 inhabitants, and the impression of emptiness is increased by the fact that more than half the population is concentrated in a few big towns. In the almost complete absence of a native population it would have been a simple matter to import a labour army of Kanaks, Polynesians, Chinese or Japanese, but the Australians are unwilling to adopt such a solution because they wish to keep a 'White Australia' and because their trade unions fear the competition of cheap labour used to a lower standard of life. The few attempts which were made to use Kanak labour on the sugar plantations and Chinese labour in the mines were not persisted with, and gradually all these non-Whites have been deported. The result is that the population of Australia is homogeneous, but at the same time all work of whatever nature, including the humblest and most arduous, has to be performed by Whites. Seeing that all these white workers naturally demand a Western standard of living, even an American standard of living, wages are high and living in general is correspondingly affected.

A number of important consequences result. First of all the Australian must engage in labour: he must go into the factories and work with his hands, and he must work again at home to keep the household going because the help available is reduced to a strict minimum by the labour shortage. To a certain extent this is satisfactory, because it means that labour, even manual labour, is highly esteemed. However, we know from experience that in almost all countries the hardest work is done by the more humble immigrants, as it was formerly done by the humbler elements from the country districts. In France we have Italians and Spaniards doing this work, and in the nineteenth century there was a whole class of domestic servants who came from the outlying provinces. In the United States it is done by coloured people and by the humbler European immigrants.

The Frenchman and the American tend to avoid this arduous kind of work, but in Australia it has to be done by the Australians themselves since they regard any coloured immigration with suspicion, even immigration from the Mediterranean countries, fearing that it might depress their standards of living. The result is that certain work is either too dear to have done, or is not done because no one is willing to do it.

In Queensland I have seen white workers cutting sugar cane under a broiling sun for 10/- a day, whereas coloured workers would have done it with much less effort and at a fraction of the cost. In such circumstances the authorities must grant subsidies if sugar is to be made available at reasonable prices. I was also told that certain deep mines cannot be worked because Australian miners are not willing to undertake the very heavy labour involved. Thus the economic development of Australia is being limited and hampered. Is it really worth while to pay that price in order to escape the colour problem?

Let us return to South Africa. The country has all the advantages which come from the possession of slaves, or at least serfs, or if you prefer, just backward proletarians. The mines profit from the existence of a large and cheap army of coloured labour (400,000 coloured workers are employed in the gold and diamond workings). Domestic labour is also plentiful, and everyone, including the white workers, is waited upon by coloured servants. On the farms the hard work — I could almost say simply the work — is performed by a depressed population of coloured workers whose wages amount to next to nothing. The Union of South Africa would find itself in an extremely awkward situation if this army of cheap labour power were suddenly withdrawn from one day to the next. It is quite true that apart from being cheap it is also relatively inefficient, and this naturally increases the costs of production. It is also true (and we shall return to the point later) that the white trade unions — with the backing of public opinion incidentally — deliberately prevent the coloured worker from improving his technical standard, which he is quite capable of doing. In such circumstances production necessarily works under a handicap.

It should be added, too, that the employment of coloured labour power, whether slave or free, demoralizes the White. He gets used to not working with his hands and finally he even comes to despise manual labour, believing that the function of a superior race is simply to direct the labour of others. Children in South Africa are accustomed to being waited on rather as Americans were at one time in the Southern States. Also because the coloured man is not represented in the legislative assembly, and South African legislation gives a privileged position to the White, the latter easily grows accustomed to treating the coloured people with contempt. It can be suggested, too, that because the question of defence against the coloured people occupies all energies and all political activities (in particular those of the white workers, who are highly paid and privileged), progressive political parties do not come into being, with the result that countries so constituted lag behind the general political development of the Western world.

And finally, life in South Africa is overshadowed by fear, a vague feeling of fear difficult to describe, the the fear of being overwhelmed by numbers in the long run and submerged in what an American writer has called 'the rising tide of colour'. Australia suffers from the same fear, but for her the danger threatens from outside and she seeks to protect herself by erecting an artificial barrier, the immigration laws. The Union of South Africa is threatened from within.

Let us leave the question I raised a little while back: which is better off, Australia or South Africa, or at least which suffers · the lesser disadvantage? Wisdom advises me not to attempt an answer at present.

# CHAPTER IX

# THE COLOUR PROBLEM
## IN THE TRANSVAAL (2)

IN this 'Land of problems' the colour problem is by far the gravest and most urgent, and I shall not be exaggerating if I add, the most alarming. I have met no one who did not speak of it with pessimism, more for the future than for the present. The problem arises in different ways in different parts of the country. In the Transvaal it refers chiefly to the Negro population; in Natal it is the Indians; in Cape Colony it is the Mulattos, known as 'Cape coloured'. For the moment I propose to deal only with the Transvaal, but the problem is the same in all parts of the country.

The population figures already given for the Union of South Africa are enough in themselves to indicate how serious the problem is, and it is complicated and aggravated by the fact that an industrial and capitalist civilization suddenly superimposed itself, without a transition period, on a pastoral civilization in which the coloured people had remained in an almost completely primitive state of development.

Today the question has a double aspect: it includes the relation of the coloured labourer with the Boer farmer (incidentally, the word Boer means farmer) in the countryside, and in the town and the mining districts with his white employer and with the white worker, whose competitor he threatens to become.

The White is the master, and to a great extent he

is so still even when he is himself a worker. The coloured man is the proletarian, and it is thus possible to appeal to his discontent either from the social standpoint, in the same way as to all proletarians, or from the ethnic standpoint, since he is treated as a member of an inferior race. There is some similarity here to the position of the native Indian in the Chilean mines for example, but even more so to that of the coloured worker in the Southern States of the U.S.A. In the latter case the reaction of the White to the coloured man is the same as it is in South Africa and for the same reason; it is rooted in fear and the instinct of self-defence.

The Government of the Union of South Africa has just appointed a special ambassador accredited to the world at large to defend its ethnic policy against the attacks to which it is being subjected. In many respects that policy shocks us, and in the long run it must inevitably lead to an impasse. However, this ambassador will be able to plead extenuating circumstances, and they should be taken into account when a section of the white race, instinctively feeling its future threatened, seeks to defend itself.

This vague fear which troubles a minority which has no real chance of increasing its numerical strength is rather pathetic. In the United States the presence of 13,000,000 coloured people in a total population of 145,000,000 is embarrassing, troublesome, even grave, but it in no way threatens the future of our Western civilization. The situation is very different in South Africa, where there are four natives to one white man, and where it is manifestly impossible to hold down an allegedly inferior race indefinitely.

The attitude of the various classes of the population towards the coloured race differs according to whether the Whites in question are rural Afrikander, British employers of labour, skilled white workers, unskilled white workers, members of the reformed Dutch Church or Anglicans.

We know that the Dutch farmers emigrated to the interior when slavery was suppressed in Cape Colony. They sought an independence in the Veldt which civilization denied them. On their farms in the Transvaal and the Orange Free State they employed coloured labour under conditions which can truly be described as serfdom, and which largely continue to be so today. The Afrikander went north from the south, and from the north came the Bantus (Kaffirs, Basutos and Zulus), and a struggle took place for possession of the land, a struggle in which in the long run the coloured tribes were defeated. But both sides can claim that the land belongs to them; each side can treat the other as an intruder.

The Boer has developed very little in his ideas concerning the subject race. His attitude is that of the American in the Southern States: there is no equality between the White and the man of colour; the latter is inferior by nature and will always remain so, and, in any case, it is necessary that he should remain so. The curse that rested on Ham continues to burden his descendants. Readers of the Bible, and in particular the Old Testament, those orthodox believers who uphold the letter of the law, do not consider that in thinking as they do they are running counter to Divine law. On the contrary, they believe that God created the difference and that it must be maintained.

Incidentally, and particularly in the rural areas, the coloured man is so far behind in civilization that his subjection appears normal and natural; children are brought up to regard him as a sort of helot who may be human, but to whom one cannot ascribe the ordinary human sentiments; something like a familiar dog for which one feels, be it said, a certain sympathy — but only on condition that he keeps his place. Should he want to raise himself, and against your wishes, then you detest him, and any weapon appears legitimate against him. It is the Boer in particular who is hostile to the advancement of the coloured people.

For different reasons the white worker arrives at a somewhat similar attitude. Coming, generally speaking, from Europe he feels no natural hostility towards the coloured race and he does not attack it except to the extent to which the coloured workman, increasing his technical competence, threatens to compete with him and undercut him; but once that competition begins to be felt, or even begins to threaten remotely, his reaction is immediate and uncompromising. Later on we shall study this question from the economic standpoint, but we can already say that the white workers tend to adopt the same attitude towards the coloured man as do the Afrikander, and most of them, in fact, are Afrikander.

The hostility is even greater amongst the unskilled white workers, men who are themselves nothing but ordinary manual labourers. For them the threat of competition from the coloured workman really is a terrible one, because their demand for higher wages would certainly be undercut by him if the law did not protect them. In fact I ask myself how in the long run they can avoid being eliminated. It is the fatal problem of the 'Poor White'.

The employer of labour is naturally not troubled by the same fear, and, as in the United States, it is not from him that the hostility to coloured labour develops. As an employer he is interested in obtaining cheap labour, and he even has an interest in treating his labour well, just as a man has an interest in treating a horse well which he uses as a draught animal or for riding.

At first the coloured workmen employed in the mines were treated as a proletariat to whom no one dreamt of showing the slightest consideration (was it not very much the same a hundred years ago in Europe?). However, a change has since come about and it is important that we should take note of it.

Thus originally no one took any interest in the well-being of the coloured people. 'Am I my brother's keeper?' asked Cain. But since then the exploited race has found champions. The Englishman coming from the old country is more liberal; at least he is in principle, though individually he remains cold and distant in the presence of the man of colour, more so even than the Afrikander accustomed to long familiarity with him as a servant.

The Protestant and Catholic missionaries naturally adopted a more humane attitude, or simply a more Christian attitude, and sought to treat the man of colour as a fellow human being whose dignity must also be respected. The Anglican Church is even inclined to exaggerate the concessions which should be made to the other race, as Anglo-Saxons carried away by their convictions often are.

Communist propaganda works in the same direction, preaching racial equality and revolt, and we can observe the 'Fellow Travellers', sometimes well-to-do and often Jews, associating themselves with it; the sowers, perhaps unconsciously, of future violence.

. I should not like to omit mentioning the fact that the Native Affairs Administration, and the Municipality of Johannesburg, have a splendid personnel devoted to their work and anxious to do justice and serve the general interests.

All this does not mean that the problem is even on the way to solution. Although the left wing of the United Party shows a liberal spirit in dealing with the question, one may well wonder whether, in fact, the majority of the party does not at bottom share the fears of the National Party at the prospect of the advancement of the coloured people.

A legally established colour bar exists in the gold mines, but the colour bar is even more strongly marked in social life, where it is not one whit less virulent than in the Southern States of the U.S.A. Coloured people may live only in certain quarters and they may not move around unless they are in possession of a special 'pass'. They are excluded from hotels, restaurants and tramcars used by Whites, from places of entertainment and even from benches in the parks. No one shakes the hand of a coloured man and in address his name is never prefaced with 'Mr.' He is usually addressed by his Christian name, and at the utmost by his family name if he is an educated man. There are two different streams of humanity in South Africa and they never mingle.

And yet the two races are condemned to live side by side and they have need of each other. We must take all these circumstances into consideration when speaking of South Africa.

CHAPTER X

# WHITE AND COLOURED LABOUR
# IN SOUTH AFRICA

THE colour problem is a problem of social relations, but in addition it is a problem of rivalry between two classes of workers separated not only by their class but also by the colour of their skin, a circumstance which creates an abyss impossible to bridge.

It is all very simple. The coloured worker with his extraordinary modest requirements and his general low level of life is able to work hard in return for low wages. Naturally, employers prefer him to the white worker whenever the latter is not his superior in efficiency. This means that the coloured worker is destined to be a manual labourer, which, logically, is the status he is accorded whenever the two races meet. Equally naturally, the white worker occupies the more highly-qualified positions, and he is paid either for his technical qualifications or for his needs as a civilized man — obviously at a much higher rate. And this is exactly what happens in practice. According to official statistics for the years 1937-47, 84.1 per cent of white workers are classed as skilled workers, 16.5 per cent as semi-skilled workers, and only 2.1 per cent as unskilled workers. On the other hand, 83.2 per cent of all coloured workers are classed as unskilled, 12.7 per cent as semi-skilled and only 4.1 per cent as skilled.

In Europe complaints can be heard that the difference between the wages of skilled and unskilled workers is not big enough. In South Africa it is excessive because it corresponds not only to a difference of category, but of race. In the mines a skilled white worker receives on an average between 25/- and 30/- a day, whilst the unskilled labourer (coloured) receives 2/6 a day, though in addition he is lodged and fed, a circumstance which makes the comparison difficult. Nevertheless, the difference is enormous.

In industry in general the difference is not so great. On an average the wages of a skilled worker are twice as high as those of a semi-skilled worker and four times as high as those of an unskilled labourer. And always there are two standards, one for the white worker and the other for the coloured worker. On the farms the wages of the latter are much worse still and he lives there under conditions of semi-serfdom.

Local opinion approves these differences and regards them as normal — it would even consider it dangerous to attempt to diminish them. It would like to see the coloured people definitively, statutorily so to speak, confined to lower-grade employment, whilst all work requiring technical competence was reserved to the Whites. Statistics seem to show that this is, in fact, what is happening at present. In the gold mines the law protects the white worker in the sense that skilled employment is forbidden to the coloured worker. No such legally-established limitation applies to industry in general, but both here and there trade-union pressure tends to reserve skilled employment to 'Europeans'. This attitude of the trade unions is obstinate and intransigent but it is generally effective, so that business and employment divisions are determined not only by class differences but also by racial differences. The proletariat is coloured, which means that its social agitation is naturally reinforced by an ethnic agitation. It is this circumstance that makes the problem so grave, particularly as the coloured man is, after all, quite capable, and often desirous, of advancing his position and improving his technical ability.

It is said, and with some justice, that natives are excellent at manual labour, but that they show a marked inferiority as soon as the work becomes at all complex; that they lack the capacity to reason, to adapt themselves readily to a new situation, to take responsibility. The coloured worker can mind a machine, but if he is left to his own devices he minds it badly and there is a danger that it will deteriorate in his hands owing to carelessness.

These objections are well founded, and yet all employers of labour admit that the man of colour is capable of learning a trade and practising it usefully, and that in many cases he could replace the white worker in employment which the latter claims as his exclusive preserve. All that you need do here is to keep your eyes open both in the factories and in the outside workings to see that everything which is properly called work is performed by coloured men under the direction of white foremen, and that these latter often confine themselves to giving orders, sometimes even to merely looking on. That is not the case where skilled technique is involved, but it is so for the less difficult operations even when some measure of skill is involved.

When work is carried on in this fashion the native is quite naturally brought to develop his abilities, and it is said that in many cases if the white worker were absent his native assistants could readily take his place. This advancement of the under race is particularly noticeable where semi-skilled work is concerned, for instance on the assembly bands. Modern industry employs a growing number of workers for this kind of work and in consequence there is quite a sphere in which the coloured worker is naturally encouraged to develop his abilities, despite the trade unions but with the approval of his employer.

For a long time the gold mines represented the only industry in the country, but since the first world war, and in particular since the second, general industrial activity has developed considerably and this, too, requires a large labour force. Industrialists have therefore had to recruit not only white but also coloured workers, and in many cases they would be in competition with each other but for the fact that trade-union policy is precisely to keep a reserved domain for the 'European' worker, a sort of closed preserve.

The trade unions strive to keep the native worker confined to unskilled employment whilst the natural development of things tends to raise him above such employment to the extent to which he progresses as a result of his contact with Western civilization. In this struggle the employer is inclined to support the native worker, but public opinion is on the side of the unions, fearing that in advancing his status the coloured man might come to claim a social equality which public opinion denies him. There has not been much progress in this respect and it cannot be said that the social atmosphere in South Africa is becoming more liberal.

On reflection the question is even more disturbing

than it appears at first sight. For about fifteen years now the country has enjoyed a period of exceptional prosperity due in particular to the war, which stimulated the development of its industries. There is no unemployment, in fact, employers are constantly on the look-out for labour power, which is never in adequate supply. In such circumstances white workers, even those without any particular skill, can easily find employment.

But if there were a depression (and there can hardly fail to be one some day) these second-class Europeans, who are numerous, would find themselves in competition with natives who may be capable of doing better work, not only as manual labourers, but also as semi-skilled and even skilled workers. In any struggle in which the Whites were not protected they would inevitably be squeezed out by less pretentious competitors. And if the Whites took up the struggle with a fair field and no favour then, reduced to accepting the same wages as the coloured workers, they would have to lower their standard of living almost to the level of their rivals. It is the classic problem of the 'Poor White'. Formerly acute in South Africa, a period of prosperity has lessened its severity, but it could recur again in all its virulence and I believe that it will inevitably do so in the future.

It is, in fact, impossible in the long run to hold down a whole section of any population systematically merely on account of its colour. A still small and unimportant, but growing number of coloured people are educating themselves. The percentage of coloured people who have received an elementary education is now as great as it was for Whites fifty years ago.

Public opinion in South Africa, fanatical in its determination to keep down the coloured race, is disturbed by this development more than by anything else.

Whenever proposals are made to give technical training to coloured workers, there is spontaneous and instinctive opposition, and as the man of colour is not represented on any authoritative body and as he is obstinately opposed by the trade unions, which have become simple defenders of their privileges, his interests are upheld only by humanitarian circles, Communists and their sympathizers (possible trouble-makers), and thoughtful politicians who feel that the colour bar, though understandable and even to some extent justifiable, cannot be maintained in its present form indefinitely without the risk of grave disorders and an ethnic revolution in a future perhaps not so far distant as one might think.

It is really not astonishing that such a situation has developed in a country which was formerly pastoral and which was then suddenly overwhelmed by the Western-European nineteenth century in its most aggressive form so that a mechanical intruder civilization without any natural counter-checks came into contact with a native race which was not merely backward but actually primitive.

The 'industrial revolution' here produced all the same results as it did a hundred years ago in our old continent, but in addition the social problem was complicated by the colour problem, and that makes it of alarming gravity.

# CHAPTER XI

# UPROOTED NATIVES IN JOHANNESBURG

JOHANNESBURG is one of the most modern towns, even one of the most aggressively modern towns, in the world; although it cannot be said to have existed for more than fifty years, to be in it is to have a sense of the past. The social problems existing there recall those of the industrial revolution at the beginning of the nineteenth century in England, when manufacturers who grew up with the steam engine emptied the countryside in their demand for labour, and the towns swallowed up masses of people like insatiable ogres. The gold mines of South Africa exercised an equally strong pull on the white worker coming from outside and on the coloured man leaving his reservation and abandoning his old tribal life. This movement of man-power has been so rapid that urban amenities, and housing and accommodation generally, have constantly lagged behind current needs, the more so because — again as was the case at the beginning of the nineteenth century in Europe — very little consideration was shown as a rule to the quasi-anonymous workers; this indifference was the greater because they were largely of another race. The great shift of population came about without any ordered direction or foresight and purely in accordance with the interests of employers of labour, and it was only gradually that consideration for the general interests and for ordinary humanity began to make itself felt amongst mine managements and in the municipality, upon which the task of accommodating this human tidal wave devolved. The development of industries born of war-time exigencies aggravated the severity of the problem.

In 1946 Johannesburg had 777,416 inhabitants of whom 395,231 were coloured. Within the space of ten years the coloured population had increased to 72 per cent of the whole, and it is now estimated that Johannesburg has over half a million coloured inhabitants. Their numbers are recruited both from the surrounding countryside and from neighbouring colonies, particularly Portuguese Mozambique.

In the country districts, either in their own reservations or working on the farms as servants and labourers of the Whites, the natives live a life of extreme poverty. The soil, recklessly overtaxed by extensive tilling and stock-breeding, is exhausted and threatened with erosion, and it is hardly able to feed the native population which lives on it, usually in very miserable huts but at least under conditions which still preserve the old traditions of tribal life. When they migrate to the towns these natives lose their roots and raise the gravest social problems. Now we must distinguish several stages and various characteristics in this human flood.

Recruitment for the mines is in a class of its own. The mines need a big labour force and, as far as the natives are concerned, an unskilled force, and the chief thing required of it is that it shall, in fact, be cheap. Without the 400,000 natives it employs the mining industry would have been unable to develop satisfactorily or, incidentally, to maintain its prosperity.

Only single men are recruited, usually for a limited period — six or nine months. After that they return to their village having accumulated enough money to buy a wife or wives — according to their tribal traditions it is the man who provides the dowry, so to speak.

The coloured miner is lodged and fed. He lives in a special area known as a compound. He is permitted to go outside it and to move around freely, but only with a special pass, because the segregation of the coloured race is strictly controlled. Some of these compounds are modern, clean and well planned, but others are old and make a painful impression on the observer; in these latter men sleep forty or sixty in one dormitory in tiered bunks. Generally speaking the native worker is quite well fed; obviously it is in the interests of his employer to maintain his physical efficiency, and the food he gets when working in the mines is certainly better than he is accustomed to in his village.

Whilst visiting these compounds, some of which contain several thousand natives, I asked myself just what it is that shocks the visitor. It is not the physical treatment of the native, which is quite good, but rather the fact that he is confined to these compounds, and, above all, the fact that he receives such a very small and obviously disproportionate share of the yield of the gold mines. In itself the system is not socially bad because it does not 'de-tribalize' the native, and it allows him to return to his tribe, where he once again finds a social organization in accordance with his traditions and the needs of his own development.

The question becomes more complicated when

subsidiary industries develop around the mines, creating a multitude of new opportunities for employment. These industries also attract labour power, but the process is no longer controlled by big enterprises systematically assuming responsibility for it. The native worker employed by these auxiliary industries finds a lodging for himself where he can, often bringing his family with him. At first perhaps his family is not large, but it soon grows. He is still not cut off from contact with his village and he is often visited by his former associates. In accordance with native customs he will often find a whole family of parasites coming to sponge on him. Because of the South African law of racial segregation, the native can live only in certain 'locations' allotted to him.

The result is that enormous native towns spring up spontaneously on the outskirts of the White town. They form rapidly, and without any sort of order or urban planning, into conglomerations of houses run up by reckless jerry-builders devoid of social conscience, and the native is exploited by Indians, or even by other natives, who squeeze as much out of him as they possibly can. The Alexandra and Orlando quarters on the outskirts of Johannesburg are growths of this kind. In the Alexandra quarter more than 80,000 natives are huddled together in miserable shacks on a space not much more than a square mile in area. The streets are not paved and as there is no proper drainage sewage water runs away in dirty streams. There is no lighting system. To get to work a native must often walk miles. No one is properly responsible for such communities, but charitable institutions, both Christian and Jewish, do what they can to open clinics, churches and clubs and provide the women and children with various amenities.

In the same way squatters' quarters arise, that is to say, quarters of people without proper rights. They flood into the town quicker than accommodation can be found for them. Very often they come without definite employment in view, drawn merely, as everywhere else in the world, by the attraction of the big city. The shacks that are run up in such circumstances are of the worst possible type and people live on top of each other in them like sardines in a tin. The municipality is trying to clear away these squatters' quarters, which are hotbeds of crime, disorder and potential revolution, but it is not very successful, and it is not likely to be unless alternative accommodation is built.

In Johannesburg the municipal administration is now building accommodation suitable for this native population, which is definitely becoming de-tribalized in the sense that it will never again leave the town. Brick buildings of three rooms and a kitchen are going up, each to house a family, so that here conditions will henceforth be satisfactory. The municipality has also opened hostels for single men which are the equivalent of the compounds. It has even set up a special quarter where the native artisan can ply his trade in accordance with his traditions. I paid a visit to this quarter and found carpenters, metal workers, leather workers and so on at their tasks. Although the surroundings are urban, the atmosphere is exotic. There are in particular numerous shops kept by herbalists; strange personages, very much like sorcerers, who sell amulets, magic barks, herbs, pieces of skin and horn. An attempt is thus being made to preserve native traditions, but can it succeed?

The native loves the town, the noise, the society of his fellows and the general communal life, provided however that he can still live a private family life behind the walls of his little house. Thus a whole native population is forming which has lost its original roots. When such natives live in unsatisfactory conditions, all the evils of the big town inevitably arise: robbery, crime and vagabondage on the part of young people and even children. In certain quarters it is dangerous to venture out after dark, even for natives. Communist, or simply anti-White, propaganda is certain of finding a ready response, particularly as the coloured man, a good fellow but immature and highly emotional, is easily stimulated by all sorts of incitement.

The standpoint of the Nationalist Party is that segregation must be maintained and even more strictly enforced. That standpoint is fundamentally reasonable because neither the white man nor the coloured really wishes to live together with the other race. The doctrine of *Apartheid* envisages sending the coloured people back to their reservations where they would live their own lives, but the fact is that these reservations are incapable of feeding them all, and one may well ask whether it is not already too late to think of such a thing now that the coloured man though lacking our maturity, tends to live, and wants to live, a life analogous to our own.

If the coloured man raises himself what place can be found for him? If he becomes a skilled worker what will happen to the unskilled White? If the coloured man were given ordinary representation like the White is it not obvious that under the influence of agitators he would abuse it? And if it is proposed to keep him down can this be done indefinitely in an Africa where other natives are rapidly developing? The natives are four times as numerous as the Whites in South Africa, hence the sombre fear of the future felt by the Boers. That obsession explains, if it does not justify, their intransigence. To look at the colour problem in South Africa is very much like looking over the edge of an abyss.

# CHAPTER XII

# SOUTH AFRICA HAS AN INDIAN PROBLEM TOO

IT was at Bulawayo, in Southern Rhodesia, coming from the Atlantic, that I met the first Indians, as we must apparently call them. I had the feeling of passing into another continent. The presence of India, the immense India of 400,000,000 inhabitants, was manifest.

Ethnically speaking India outruns her frontiers. She is invading the whole eastern coast of Africa. The result is an Indian problem, an ethnic, economic and social one which may in addition become a political one with the existence of Hindustan and Pakistan as independent States in the constellation of powers. The problem can be met with in Kenya and Mozambique; it disturbs South Africa and it is virulent in Durban. Even Madagascar is not exempt.

There are 285,000 Asiatics in the Union of South Africa or 2.5 per cent of the population. That is not very much, but 228,000 of them live in Natal alone, where they represent 10.4 per cent of the total population; and in Durban, the great harbour town of Natal, there are 113,000 out of a total population of 358,000, that is to say 31.5 per cent. At the same time there are 125,000 Europeans or 34.8 per cent, 109,000 natives, or 30.6 per cent, and 10,000 Mulattos. Now Asiatics are much more prolific than Europeans, and they will soon be more numerous — if they are not so already —

than Whites in Durban, a town which is proud of its European character and its white civilization.

There were not always Asiatics in these parts. They were first imported from India by the colony of Natal in 1860 to serve as labourers on the sugar plantations. These immigrants were engaged under contract for five years in conditions approximate to serfdom (indentured labour). After they had served their time they could sign on for another period. If they were unwilling to do so they could remain in the colony as free settlers, or they could be repatriated. The majority of them preferred to remain, not on the plantations, but as workers in industry, as farm labourers and traders.

Together with this collective importation of indentured labourers for the sugar plantations there developed an uncontrolled and unorganized immigration of traders, chiefly Moslems (the imported labourers were usually Hindus), who lived to a great extent by exploiting their compatriots. In this way a class of rich Indians developed, the owners of big shops, but the mass of the immigrants remained poor and their standard of living was hardly better than that of the native population. The Indian quarters are overcrowded, accommodation is inadequate and there are many hovels. It is estimated that two-thirds of this Asiatic population have barely sufficient for their minimum requirements.

The Indian problem thus appears as a problem of pauperism. It was clearly born of a development too rapid to allow social progress to keep pace with it, and at the same time the municipality has not treated these Indians as it would have treated Whites. At the other extreme there is another Indian problem which arises because some Indians are very rich, and they surreptitiously invade positions reserved for the Whites. On the one hand the white population sees itself compelled to relieve Asiatic pauperism out of the municipal taxes, whilst on the other it feels compelled to defend itself against the passive infiltration of Indian businessmen who are singularly adroit and enterprising.

When we think of Indians we think of Gandhi, and we are generally inclined to forget that India is a country where the sense for bargaining is extraordinarily acute. The Indian has a genius for trading. He is insinuating, crafty and indefatigable. His personal needs are modest and he accumulates his profits, becoming rich, sometimes very rich, even richer than many white men. His principal, almost his only investment, is in land. He buys himself land and a house, which he then proceeds to furnish luxuriously, but he lives in only one or two of the rooms, a habit which we know quite well in our Midi. He can be seen being driven around in American luxury cars, and when he appears Greeks and Jews recoil before him. He is by no means self-effacing and he makes his presence felt, particularly as he is argumentative, litigious and determined to have his rights. And then by nature the Indian is a large-family man. In Durban the mortality rate for white people is 2 per cent, for Indians it is 4.4 per cent. But although his mortality rate (and particularly his infant mortality rate) is much higher than that of the white man, his numbers increase twice as fast.

Immigration from India has now been stopped, but

it is already too late; the simple operation of that prolific birth-rate is sufficient to make the presence of the Indian all pervasive and dangerous. And the Indian is dangerous not only on account of his numbers, but also on account of his ability. India is an old country; in her tradition of civilization at least our equal, in some respects even our superior in the domain of thought. Unlike the South African native, the Indian is by no means primitive.

In such circumstances one can easily see to what extent his presence is a danger. There is a well-founded fear that, becoming more numerous than the white men, the Indians might displace them: by means of the vote if it were accorded to them, and even more so by surreptitiously buying up businesses, land and shops.

If, on the other hand, the Indian community is left in a state of poverty, that is a source of trouble too: of international protests, for instance, because Indians are adept at stirring up world public opinion, all the more so now that the two Dominions of India have become political powers determined to take their place in the concert of nations.

At first, when the workers on the sugar plantations were simple proletarians with dark skins, there was no such problem. When it finally arose the Whites began to defend their interests, and various measures were adopted, including discrimination against Indians, who were forbidden to acquire or occupy land and houses in certain areas reserved for white people, and found themselves confined to certain other areas on municipal territory.

But that was not all; a colour bar just as implacable

as any which exists in the Southern States of the U.S.A. places the Indians outside the pale of the privileged white race. Even educated and cultured Indians may not use hotels, restaurants, cinemas, trams or trains patronized by white people.

Worse still, the law effectively prevents their children from receiving the technical training which would open skilled trades to them. The aim is to keep them, like the natives, to unskilled employment.

The Indian, particularly when he is cultured, bitterly resents this state of affairs. He is refused the right to vote and he is legally forbidden to raise himself in the social scale. 'Why is this?' he asks. 'Am I not a civilized man?' That may be true, but ethnically and even socially he remains an Indian. The men dress as we do, but not the women, and, generally speaking, they do form an exotic community, an enclave in a Western community. It is a cruel problem and it is difficult to see the solution.

It is clear that some form of municipal or political representation is necessary. 'But,' the Whites reply, 'if the Indians were in a majority we should have an Indian mayor. And if one day all landed property passed into the hands of these men of another race we should no longer be able to call our town our own.'

The big towns in Eastern America have experienced similar invasions of Greeks and Italians, but at least these are white. Here the colour is the difficulty.

The problem is made particularly embarrassing and alarming because by the mediatory action of India it has been brought before U.N.O. and the I.L.O., that is to say, it has been submitted to the judgment of the world.

Fifty years ago the problem of the *Uitlander*, that is to say, of those Englishmen who were established as foreigners in the Boer Republics, was not so very much different in aspect, but that at least was a quarrel between Whites. When two races differing in colour are involved matters become much more serious and complicated. U.N.O. has no means of exercising pressure on South Africa apart from moral suasion, but if later on India became an effective political power capable of expansion and intervention then the problem would change in character and become extremely disturbing for a country like South Africa with a population of only two and half million Whites, a small European island in a rising sea of colour.[1]

[1] The rioting which took place in Durban in January 1949 stressed the gravity of this Indian problem.   A. S.

# CHAPTER XIII

## 'POOR WHITES'

IN societies based on slavery the 'Poor White' is one who possesses neither land nor slaves. Employers prefer servile labour to his because it is cheaper, and so, unless he possesses some particular technical skill, he is reduced to idleness and charity, or emigration. If he abandons himself passively to such a situation he soon slides into chronic pauperism and social decay. Under a less virulent form the problem of the 'Poor White' continues to exist wherever white workers and coloured workers compete with each other. The Union of South Africa is not exempt. Though the prosperity enjoyed in recent years has greatly diminished its gravity, the problem remains latent. I believe that it would recur actively in the event of an economic crisis.

The 'Poor White' and the 'de-tribalized' native are two products of the same agrarian problem. Apart from her mineral resources, South Africa is really a poor country. Although parts of her territory are fertile, the soil does not lend itself readily to cultivation and yields are always uncertain. The economy tends, on the whole, to be pastoral. In addition, the primitive methods of the Boer farmers, who are nomads at heart with little understanding of soil conservation, have created a condition of partial erosion. Land which was once fertile has been deprived of its top-soil and now tends to become waste. It follows that the land can no longer feed its population, and a part, both white and coloured, is emigrating into the towns where mining and other industries offer employment.

After the great migration of the nineteenth century towards the uplands of the Orange Free State and the Transvaal, the Boer farmers established themselves on vast farms, some of them tens of thousands of acres in extent. They were days of ease, and farmers tilled their land only to support their families; the rest was chiefly stock-breeding. Practically all the work was done by native labourers, who were in reality slaves, and the farmer and his children contented themselves with the mere direction of their labours.

However, the population increased, both by new migrations and by the natural process of birth, and soon there was no more land available. As in France, there was no law of primogeniture and in consequence the farms, once enormous, became smaller and smaller until finally they proved insufficient to support their owners.

Some of them continued to live miserably on what remained of their lands. Others established themselves as *Bywoner*, that is to say as tolerated occupiers without title on the fringe of farms which had remained large. But, accustomed hereditarily to make the native work for them, these men were, generally speaking, incapable of any serious effort. Miserable enough themselves, they nevertheless continued to live on the labour of a few natives even more miserable. They had been demoralized by the servile tradition of their lives, and they continued to regard any form of manual labour as a social shame. Work to them was 'Kaffir's business', and they sank lower and lower into

decay caused by a false pride which made them
indolent. Some of them even sank so low that they
lived in conditions very little better than those of the
natives.

These social degenerates are prolific, and after a
time the size of their families made migration into the
towns imperative. Not only had they no trade and no
particular skill but they were not even accustomed to
working. Before long they found themselves in competition with the natives, who were no more skilled
than they were but whose labour was cheaper. If the
White then agreed to accept the same wages as the
native worker he sank to his social level, and if he
refused to do so he condemned himself to chronic
unemployment in conditions often just as degrading,
that is to say, he condemned himself to what we used
to call pauperism. Logically therefore every White
who was incapable of skilled employment fell into
indigence, and the mentality developed by an inbred
habit of looking to others to wait upon him caused him
to sink still deeper into the social mire because even
in his misery there were certain things he refused to do.
He regarded all manual work as beneath his dignity,
particularly work in the household. In the worst
hovels people living on nothing but public charity
still had native women to clean their floors and do their
washing. It is a process of degeneration, and some
people attribute it to persistent interbreeding, but it
derives, too, and in a direct line, from slavery, or at
least from the serfdom which survived it. These people
are humanity's rejects.

Twenty years ago an investigation of the International Labour Office estimated the number of these

Whites without a trade and without any regular occupation at several hundred thousand. Even today all big towns in South Africa can still produce numerous examples of the breed. They are jealous of the natives and they are not without influence because, unlike the natives, they have the vote. Politicians therefore treat them with consideration. 'You are aristocrats', announced an important politician at a meeting of these unemployables; and they are, in fact, very much like the sons of ruined families: they have come down in the world, but they are still pretentious in their fashion.

Today the problem they once created has lost much of its sting and I mention it only because I believe that it can one day reappear for the same reasons which produced it originally. For various causes (which I shall have occasion to discuss later) the Union of South Africa has experienced a period of exceptional prosperity since 1934. It has rapidly become industrialized, and even today new factories are still being built everywhere. In consequence there is still a great demand for labour, and because of the new methods of large-scale industrial production it is primarily a demand for semi-skilled workers. Thus the 'Poor Whites' of yesterday now find it comparatively easy to find employment for which they need no special competence. Certainly they find themselves having to compete with natives, and in particular with Mulattos (who are called 'coloured' in South Africa), but there is still room for them all.

In addition, the Nationalist governments which were in power before the war, and the Herzog Cabinet in particular, were anxious to favour this class of

Whites, who are primarily Afrikander, and they systematically employed them in undertakings controlled by the State, particularly on the railways, where, to the exclusion of the natives, they were used for a multiplicity of tasks which were classed as skilled, but which in reality were nothing of the sort. Thanks to this, and to industrial and military recruitment, very many of the distressed Whites of yesterday have been extricated from their misery and once again given a place in the ordered structure of society.

However, I cannot feel that the solution is definitive. Should there be an economic depression lasting for any considerable length of time the problem would arise again, and in the same terms as before. Normally speaking the coloured man is paid less because his needs are less, and when the White can offer no superiority whatever (and not everyone can be superior) he runs the risk of being ignored by employers. During the past few years that would often have been his lot but for the fact that in a dozen and one ways, some frank and others hypocritical, the law or the unions give him privileges merely on account of the fact that he is a 'European'. An apprenticeship law, whose real significance extends much further than its mere title would imply, prevents the native and the Mulatto from obtaining the technical training which could turn them into dangerous competitors. Semi-skilled labour represents an intermediate sphere in which the employer can, at a pinch, employ the coloured workman in conditions which are rather better than these in which a whole social system is determined to keep him.

Thus the unskilled white worker is able to keep his

head above water for the time being because on the one hand the prevailing period of prosperity favours him, and on the other he enjoys effective social protection. The return of less favourable circumstances would once again lay bare the latent weakness of the inferior elements of our race. Wherever similar conditions exist the 'Poor White' problem inevitably arises. Even though the question does not touch us directly, it is one of those whose importance we should not fail to recognize.

# CHAPTER XIV

# CAPETOWN

FOR many years the reputation of Capetown made me anxious to see a town so celebrated for the beauty of its environment, but I was still uncertain as to its appearance: 'Mediterranean', said some; 'Oceanic', said others. When I was away from Europe such comparisons made me thoughtful. Can I honestly say there was no deception at all in them? The situation of the town seems to me one of the most beautiful in the world. Can I put myself right with both my informants and say that the town is Mediterranean in so far as it faces towards the east and the Indian Ocean, and Oceanic in so far as it looks towards the west and that ocean which we, too, share? From that double angle this African town is not so totally foreign to us, as Europeans.

It has always seemed to me that in geography orientation is an essential factor of climate and colour and the character of places: a room which looks out towards the sun is sunny. In such a spirit Conrad showed, in a magnificent piece of writing, that the west wind is everywhere the same, and the east wind too. The central parts of Capetown lie at the foot of the famous Table Mountain which towers above them in a sheer wall 3500 feet high; to the west the beaches give on to the Atlantic, whilst towards the east it is the air of the Indian Ocean which gives the countryside its atmosphere.

When you arrive you think first of a colonial city,

but a colonial city of the past, not the present. There are many old houses in the Dutch style, and relatively narrow streets, all ending either at the near-by sea or at the abrupt rocks of Table Mountain. It is neither an American town nor an English one. The natives and the Mulattos lend a touch of exoticism to the scene, whilst the presence of Malays wearing the fez reminds the traveller that not far away the sea route turns towards the East and Asia. This last stage of the Atlantic Ocean can also be regarded as the first stage of the Indian Ocean. With Diaz and Vasco da Gama we look back here on quite a respectable number of centuries.

Whilst the sea, the bay, Table Mountain and Devil's Peak remind us of Naples because of the bold outlines of the mountainous slopes and also because of the perfect symmetry of the bay with sandy shores towards the north, we might also think of Toulon dominated by its proud rock. But a few minutes in the car, and the streets which lead to the west change into an ocean boulevard bordering an immense sea with splendid waves breaking perpetually on a rocky coast surmounted by high yellow mountains. And then we are reminded of Biarritz and Hendaye. It is the same blue sea inclining into green, the same wet slopes, and the same Atlantic clouds rolling slowly towards the heights and clinging there. It is easy to recognize our own Atlantic; it is still the same though it is now so far away from our home.

But if instead of going towards the west we go to the other side, skirting the escarpment of Table Mountain, we immediately find a different atmosphere. To the north there is a great plain beyond which the moun-

tains can be seen against the sky. Then to the south-
east there is the unexpected white and sandy line of
another shore, that of False Bay, which no longer
belongs to the Atlantic but to the Indian Ocean,
because Capetown is at the northern extremity of a
narrow peninsula which ends in the Cape of Good
Hope. The vegetation here is Mediterranean. The
eucalyptus shares its reign with the most beautiful
stone pines in the world amidst an abundance of semi-
tropical mimosa and magnolias and all the trees of
our Midi. And amongst them, in long well-planted
avenues, are vigorous oaks which when I saw them in
the early days of a southern spring, were just showing
their first young leaves. On the rocky soil of the mountain whose sombre-lined sides rise abruptly here, there
are green slopes, almost bucolic, reminiscent of Greece,
of the flanks of Lycabettos, of some Olympus of the
southern hemisphere.

At the Cecil Rhodes Monument and again at his
famous residence de Groote Schuur, one is reminded
almost against one's will of some conventional landscape painted by Puvis de Chavannes, though the
colours are deeper and more sombre.

The monument itself, high up on the mountainside
and dominating all the plain, is a simple white colon-
nade in the Greek style, but the house, set in the
middle of an Italianate park bordered by rows of
stone pines, is built in the style of an old Dutch residence, all white, with gables, terraces and wings which
give it the aspect of a palace despite a certain stressed
simplicity. The view of the mountain which rises
above it is of infinite nobility. One feels that a great
spirit, whatever his great faults, conceived this ensemble.

Rhodes had this place built for himself when he was Prime Minister of Cape Colony, but he left it to his official successors, and today it is Malan, the head of the National Afrikander Party, who occupies it during the sittings of parliament. Thus the house, already historic, has acquired a tradition. The library of the great imperialist is still in his study, preserved just as it was, and it contains many valuable books on Africa; in the billiard room (with a huge English table) there is a map of the continent with the original sketch of that famous route from the Cape to Cairo, which Rhodes conceived as the line of Britain's advance to the north.

What a contrast there is between the severity of the Transvaal plains, whose lines are simplified into a sort of desert purity, and the full emotional riches of this countryside, almost romantic in its Hellenic classicism! It was from here that the powerful imagination of Rhodes turned towards the far away north, 'my north', as he called it, whose great promise seemed charged with a kind of mystic attraction for him. Today, now that the destiny of the continent seems fixed, at least for the time being, Capetown has again become a maritime port in accordance with its initial tradition, a stage on the old route to the Orient opened up by the Portuguese explorers. It recalls Europe and, in particular, the Portugal, both Atlantic and Mediterranean, from which Vasco da Gama set sail. But it also previsages India. 'Cap Espoir des Indes', exclaimed the great explorer. 'Cap des Tempêtes', exclaimed Bartolomeo Diaz before him. Is it hope or fear an awakened India now inspires?

# CHAPTER XV

# THE 'CAPE COLOURED'

SOUTH AFRICAN statistics distinguish 'Europeans', natives, Asiatics (Indians in particular) and 'coloured' or half-breeds. Perhaps we ought to say Mulattos, for most of them, though not all, are the result of unions between Europeans and Negroes. As has been stated in an earlier chapter the Union of South Africa had in 1946 a total population of 11,392,000 of whom 928,000 were 'coloured' in this sense, as against 7,805,000 natives, that is to say the original coloured people of the country, 2,373,000 Europeans and 285,000 Indians. This 'coloured' group thus represents only 9.5 per cent of the population, but they are almost all in Cape Province, and in Capetown itself they represent between 40 and 50 per cent of the population.

These half-breeds, who are sometimes called 'Cape coloured', represent a mixture of many different races: native slaves from Angola and other parts of Africa; Malay slaves imported in the seventeenth and eighteenth centuries by the Dutch East Indies Company; Hottentots; Bushmen; natives from India; and Europeans. These heterogeneous unions mostly took place in the early period of European colonization when colour prejudice, a comparatively recent notion, either did not yet exist or at least was by no means so strong as it has since become. These people will no doubt continue to exist, but they are chiefly a heritage of the past, though they are none the less present and visible on that account, particularly in Capetown where they are almost as numerous as the white element.

There is a 'coloured' problem, just as there is a colour problem. Whilst we are on this subject it is interesting to note that by this South African definition many, and perhaps most, of the Negro population of the United States are 'coloured'. It is enough to look at the shade of their skins to realize that this is true. However, in the United States 'coloured' people, whether Mulattos or Negroes, form a group of their own distinct from the Whites, whilst amongst themselves there are no distinguishing lines except nuances in shade. In South Africa, however, 'coloured' people and natives form two distinct groups. The 'coloured' do not mix with the natives, and the latter have no wish to mix with them, whilst both groups are equally rigorously excluded from the white world. The problem of these 'coloured' people is a special one, but it is none the less quite troublesome.

Now whilst the natives have a tongue, or tongues, of their own and a certain primitive civilization whose traditions they have inherited and which they are losing only by degrees, these half-breeds are completely without roots.

They speak only English or Cape Dutch. They live as Europeans live though on an inferior level and they have no alternative existence. There is nothing picturesque about their quarters in Capetown, which have no character of their own. They are just the quarters of poor people or, at least, of people in modest circumstances; the houses are no different from European houses. They have all rejected the ancient religions of their native forefathers, and they are now Christian; oftentimes they are very religious, attaching great importance to a scrupulous observance of all religious customs. In this respect they can be much more readily compared with the 'coloured' people of the United States than with African natives. The problem of their social position is not made any easier by the fact that the colour bar seeks to force them towards a coloured race with which they have no desire to mingle.

In Cape Province, where almost nine-tenths of them live, their conditions are rather more liberal than those of the natives. Subject to certain property qualifications they vote like Whites and with the Whites. However, whilst white women have the right to vote, 'coloured' women have not. Further, although these 'coloured' people can vote they are not themselves eligible for election except to municipal and provincial councils. However, as a group they are in a position to affect the balance of the parties by voting for one side or the other. In practice they almost all vote for the party of Field Marshal Smuts and against Malan and his nationalist Afrikander. The latter, who are now in power, have indicated their intention of depriving these 'coloured' people of the franchise, and if they do the majority in a number of constituencies will then be nationalist Afrikander.

In the United States, or at least in the Northern States (for example, in New York), 'coloured' people have the same political and civil rights as the Whites, but they are separated by an implacable social barrier in such a fashion that the problem is far from solved, although, legally speaking, there is not much left to demand or obtain. It is much the same in South Africa. The 'coloured' people exercise their right to vote certainly, but they are not received in hotels or restaurants frequented by Whites. Up till recently they were able to travel in the same compartments as Whites in trains, at least in local trains, but now the Malan Government has decided to compel them to travel in separate compartments like the 'Jim Crow' compartments in the Southern States. They can justly claim that their conduct is exemplary and that many of them are well educated and highly civilized people, but all that is of no importance; they are rigidly excluded nevertheless. Here is perhaps the most alarming aspect of the problem: the man of colour is not most feared when he is inferior in civilization, but when he raises his level of civilization, for then he is feared as a virtual competitor who might soon declare: 'After all, I am your equal.'

Mrs. Sarah Millin, a South African author of very considerable talent, has written a novel entitled *God's Step-Children* on this subject and it is one of the best novels I have ever read. The story is pathetic. In the first half of the nineteenth century an English missionary, an idealist, discouraged by his lack of success in winning the confidence of the Hottentots, decides to marry a coloured woman. He dies, miserable, half disillusioned and still wholly misunderstood by his coloured brethren. He leaves a daughter behind as the result of his union with his coloured wife. This girl lets herself be seduced by a colonist of German origin by whom she has a son. This young man is hardly 'coloured' any longer, but the colour bar implacably forces him to join those of a similar origin to himself and he marries a 'coloured' girl by whom he has a daughter. This daughter is white and, protected by a rich neighbour, she is able to go to a school for young ladies of the superior race because her origin is kept secret. Unfortunately she falls seriously ill and the school authorities summon her parents. When they arrive the secret of her origin is revealed and she has to leave. A little later her protector manages to secure her entrance into a school a long way away, in Capetown, where a young White falls in love with her and wishes to marry her. But his family demand information about her antecedents, and when they obtain it the door is once again closed. In the end the girl's protector marries her himself and they have a child who is also quite white. However, he knows his origin and, having married an English girl from England and having a child by her, his conscience troubles him. Fearing that his child might not be able to adapt itself to South African society, where the thin strain of 'coloured' blood might be suspected, he takes his wife and child to England where he becomes a missionary and then returns to South Africa to spend his life with the natives. Thus in the end all avenues were closed and it was only as the most intimate secret of one man that the colour bar reappeared.

I am told that the book reflects reality; that reality is very painful, because no progress towards a solution of the problem can be seen — on the contrary, things are going backward, because the Nationalist Party has now declared its intention of depriving 'coloured' people of the civic rights inherited from an already distant past. However, numerous half-breeds 'pass muster', as they say in the United States; that is to say with a percentage of 'coloured' blood which has diminished almost to nothing they pass for Whites and effectively become Whites. It is generally reckoned that amongst the white population of South Africa there are many people who have 'coloured' blood in their veins, just as there are in many colonial societies. But the strain is so tenuous that it no longer counts. That solution is a happy one because it permits the acceptance of human beings who deserve to be accepted and otherwise would not be accepted. In this way indeterminate areas have been created on the frontiers of our race. But let us not forget that the main problem is still with us; that it is by no means solved; and that it does not behove us to treat it lightly either in one sense or the other.

# CHAPTER XVI

# THE CAPE ROUTE

IT is easy to see why the Cape of Good Hope has so fascinated explorers; with its extraordinary site it could not fail to do so. From Capetown towards the south a mountainous peninsula juts into the sea for about thirty-five miles between Table Bay to the north-west and False Bay to the south-east. It was no doubt at one time an island, separated from the mainland, visible to the north, by an isthmus of low-lying ground. (See Fig. 2.)

The coastal road along the Atlantic is picturesque and varied. A grand succession of bays and promontories is reminiscent of the Basque country between Biarritz and Saint Sebastian: great stretches of sand over which the Atlantic rollers break ceaselessly, and then rocky spurs overhanging the sea. The last of these great spurs in Africa is the Cape of Good Hope itself. It plunges into the sea like a sharp blade, a little curved (towards the south-east) at the point, like certain surgical instruments. Its site is one of the grandest that could possibly be imagined, partly because of the immensity of the two oceans it dominates and partly because of its exceptional position as the end of a whole continent and a groyne separating two oceans.

The Atlantic is the greener; the Indian Ocean bluer. The Atlantic is restless; the Indian Ocean more tranquil.

A glance at the map will compel us to admit that the

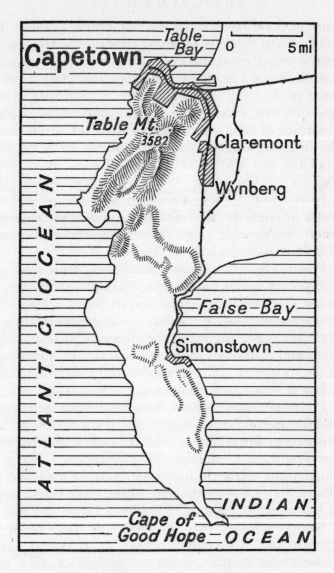

FIG 2.  THE CAPE OF GOOD HOPE

Cape of Good Hope is not the furthermost point to the south; Cape Agulhas, a little further on to the south-east, is nearer the South Pole. Nevertheless, geography has made the Cape of Good Hope the great turning point of the continent after which the mariner enters into different waters, into another part of the world: a current of cold water coming from the south chills the Atlantic, whilst a current of warm water coming from the east warms the waters of False Bay. (See Fig. 3.)

In the Middle Ages the Arabs carried spices from India through the Red Sea to Egyptian warehouses, where the Venetians took delivery to arrange for their distribution throughout the Western World.

When Vasco da Gama reached Calcutta by an unexpected route, taking the Arab-Venetian system in the rear, a page of world history was turned. The new sea route was longer, but it was unbroken by any overland stages involving the necessity of trans-shipment and it allowed sailing vessels to take advantage of the regularity of the monsoons and the trade-winds.

It was very much cheaper.

Portugal ejected Venice from her former monopoly and for several centuries after that it was no longer the Mediterranean countries but Atlantic countries like Portugal, Spain, Holland and England, which dominated trade between East and West. That state of affairs, and the predominance of the Cape route, were to last until the opening of the Suez Canal in 1869.

But even before that the nature of trade between Europe and Asia had changed its character, and towards the middle of the nineteenth century the steamship had made its appearance on the high seas.

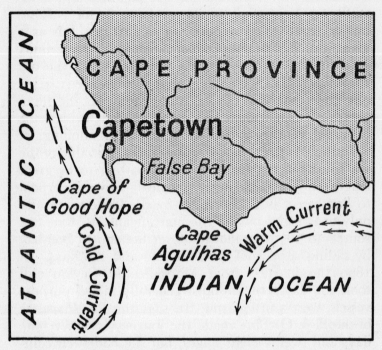

FIG. 3.  THE MEETING OF THE ATLANTIC AND THE
INDIAN OCEANS

Traders were no longer primarily interested in spices. Europe, transformed by the industrial revolution and becoming more and more densely populated, now demanded raw materials for her factories and food-stuffs for her people from overseas. Asia was no longer regarded as a purveyor of luxuries, but as a great source of useful products and, at the same time, as a market for the manufactured goods of the old continent. That complementary exchange carried out under the flag of free trade produced the nine-teenth-century system of world stability, which the twentieth century is now in course of abandoning.

In these entirely new circumstances the value of the sea route via the Cape decreased owing to its great length and its consequent slowness. From Liverpool to Bombay it is 10,680 miles by the Cape route and only 6223 miles by the Mediterranean and Red Sea route. In 1840 the journey from London to Bombay by sailing vessel took between 120 and 140 days. In 1860 the journey from Marseilles to Ceylon still took 109 days. Steamships, generally mixed purpose vessels, were a little faster. In 1842 the S.S. *Hindustan* of the P. & O. Line made the journey in ninety-one days and twenty-eight stages, but she had been com-pelled to load coal even into the saloon with the result that only a single passenger was carried.

By 1860 there had been very little progress and the voyage from Marseilles to Ceylon still took ninety-one days.

In 1854 de Lesseps had succeeded in obtaining his concession and work on the Suez Canal began. But since 1840 the fast packet boats steaming from Europe to India and back, with trans-shipment at Suez, had succeeded in shortening the journey to such an extent that the Cape route had lost its passenger trade. In 1862 my father made the journey from Toulon to Bombay in twenty days. In 1872, if I am not mistaken, Jules Verne's hero Phileas Fogg made the voyage from London to Bombay through the Suez Canal in eighteen days.

Although it was no longer used by passengers in a hurry, the Cape route still retained a certain traffic — estimated by Marius Fontanes at 60,000 in 1865 — of emigrants, mostly from England and the United States, going out to Australia, India and the Far East. It was also still favoured by sailing ships transporting heavy cargoes, cotton, linen, jute, rice, wheat, sugar, tea and coffee. The captains of these vessels would not hear of sailing through the calm seas of the Red Sea route.

In 1854 de Lesseps estimated the tonnage taking the Cape route at 6,000,000 and he hoped to be able to divert half of it through the Suez Canal. In 1869 the *Revue Contemporaine* estimated the tonnage using the Cape route as high as 11,000,000.

The objection of the sailing-ship captains was well founded, and if the steamship had not providentially won the day at about this time the building of the Suez Canal would probably have proved a failure. Lesseps came to Suez at the right time. But when he came to Panama in 1880 he was, on the other hand, twenty years too soon, for the role played by the mosquito in the dissemination of yellow fever was not discovered until the very end of the century.

The opening of the Suez Canal in 1869 is one of the great dates in the history of the world. Lesseps quite rightly appeared to the world as another Vasco da Gama. The old route via the Cape was then practically abandoned; it was used only for the transport of heavy goods of no urgency, which were still carried by sail. The time-saving economy of the new route was too obvious to be ignored: 42 per cent on the Bombay-Liverpool route; 24 per cent on the Yokohama-Liverpool route; and 8 per cent on the Melbourne-Liverpool route.

Thus the advantage offered by the Suez Canal route was decisive for the passage to India, important for the passage to the Far East, and an advantage to the passage to Australia. The circumnavigation of Africa via the Cape became an out-of-the-way, isolated and little used route. The Mediterranean route was restored to all its ancient favour. It could justly be called the life-line of the British Empire.

Quick to profit by circumstances, England, which had vigorously opposed the work of Ferdinand de Lesseps, succeeded in obtaining an influence on the Suez Canal Company in 1875 by purchasing the shares held by Ismail, and in 1882 she occupied Egypt. This represented a shift, not only in her foreign policy, but in the equilibrium of world power and the great trade routes.

To a great extent that situation belongs to the past. In competition with the Suez Canal route, and in certain cases even in preference to it, the Cape route has again become a life-line of the British world system and of the relations between East and West.

CHAPTER XVII

# SUEZ AND THE CAPE ROUTE

TWO world wars have shown that in the age of the aeroplane and the submarine the Mediterranean is no longer a safe route in the event of a European conflict. Even the possession of naval and air mastery does not mean that it can be used by shipping. Some way must be found to replace it, and in fact in 1915 and again in 1940 Great Britain turned to the Cape route for sea communications with the Indian Ocean. That represented a fundamental change in British naval policy.

By 1926 Sir John Marriot, a member of the House of Commons, could say:

'On looking at things in retrospect I am not sure that the instinct of British statesmen who opposed the Canal deceived them. If the Suez Canal had never been cut I am not sure that our position in the world today would not be better than it is. The Mediterranean is a narrow sea and the aeroplane and the submarine make it narrower still. With enemies on more than one of its shores we could experience more embarrassment than advantage from the necessity of controlling such a sea route.'

Those words were prophetic and today we can say that the Suez Canal route is no longer the life-line of the British Empire. On the other hand, the Cape route has recovered its former importance, but in new forms and under new conditions. (See Fig. 4.) The Indian Ocean remains an essential pivot of the

104

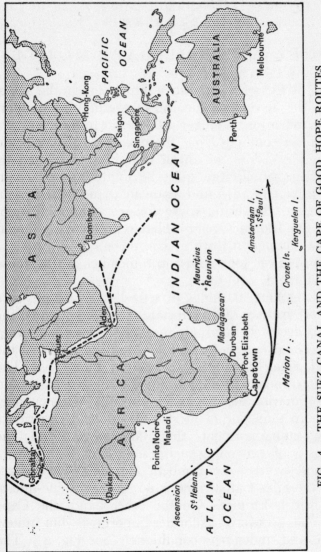

FIG. 4. THE SUEZ CANAL AND THE CAPE OF GOOD HOPE ROUTES

British system. Of course, the British are no longer in India, but for the time being at least the two Dominions of India remain within the Commonwealth, and it is of fundamental importance for the Western Powers that Russia should not get a foothold there. And then — and this is a new factor which did not exist in the nineteenth century — the petrol wells of Iraq, Persia and Arabia exhort Great Britain, the United States and ourselves not to abandon Asia, and in particular not to abandon the Persian Gulf. And finally, Great Britain is in course of building up a new colonial empire in Central and Eastern Africa.

This does not mean that she proposes to abandon the Mediterranean, but it does mean that she now considers Suez less as a passage than as an advanced post in the defence of the Middle East and the Indian Ocean. Ousted from Egypt, she maintains herself on the Canal isthmus, which the three focal points, Cyprus, Cyrenaica and Khartoum (or Abyssinia), permit her to defend effectively. However, in the event of war, maritime communications between Great Britain and the Indian Ocean would circumnavigate the Cape; and we should not forget that the roads or tracks across Africa, which were used even in the last war, are capable of considerable development.

In this constellation the old route of Vasco da Gama once again becomes essential for the relations of India with Great Britain, and also for communications with the Persian Gulf, Eastern Africa and, finally, Australia. Thus South Africa occupies a place of first-rate importance in the whole conception. The British Admiralty would find it difficult to replace Simonstown, the naval base in False Bay on the other side of the Cape of Good Hope. The base is now in the hands of Great Britain by virtue of an agreement with the government of the Union of South Africa. There is no reason to suppose that even with a Nationalist Afrikander Government in South Africa the British will not be able to remain there, but it is easy to see how necessary it is that relations between London and Pretoria should remain good. The real significance of the visit of King George VI to South Africa, which was organized by Field Marshal Smuts about three years ago, becomes clear in this light.

It is not only from the point of view of communications that South Africa is so important in this political combination; but also as the rear of a trans-African base Congo-Kenya, and as a source of industrial production in the event of a war which might put European production out of commission.

For all these reasons, the maritime route round the Cape will be of first-class importance in the event of a third world war.

After 1869 the servicing of this route was relatively neglected, but since 1914 the various ports involved have been brought up to date. Capetown (with the biggest dry dock in Africa), Port Elizabeth and Durban are particularly well equipped. In the same way, the ports of call on this route in the Atlantic and the Indian Ocean have regained the importance they once lost. St. Helena, Ascension Island, Diego Suarez, Reunion and Mauritius are all points which in the event of war, or the likelihood of war, could hardly be neglected by the interested powers.

These considerations apply primarily in the event of war, because the Suez Canal route has now recovered all its pre-war importance, but even in times of peace the circumnavigation of Africa represents to some extent a competitive route. For instance on the voyage to Australia the time saved by using the Suez Canal route is only 8 per cent, so that if prices are low and freightage cheap, and if there is no particular reason for hurry, then shippers have every reason for avoiding the heavy Suez Canal dues. To a certain extent, too, the same applies to the Far East journey, on which the time saved by using the Suez Canal route is 24 per cent. Shippers did not fail to realize the situation during the world economic crisis; for instance, in 1931 36 per cent of Australia's overseas traffic went via the Cape, and 11 per cent of all traffic to the Far East, but by 1936 these respective percentages had increased to 64 and 17. It must be remembered that when there is political tension in the Mediterranean, as there was at the time of the Spanish civil war and during the recent Palestine crisis, maritime insurance rates tend to rise for all traffic using it, and this is a factor which naturally operates in favour of the Cape route.

In these circumstances, and particularly if we take into account the recent development of western, southern and eastern Africa, it is clear that the maritime traffic round the Cape is bound to develop considerably. The ports of the Union of South Africa are kept busy first of all by the import and export trade of the Union itself, but secondly, and to quite a considerable degree, by the fact that they are situated on a maritime route which has once again become one of the great overseas routes of the world.

Ships put into Capetown to refuel with oil, to take

in water and to re-provision themselves, and they put into Durban to refuel with coal and to take in water and provisions in the same way. At the present time these two ports, and even Port Elizabeth, are experiencing a period of intense activity which is straining their loading and unloading facilities to the utmost.

Germany was well aware of the situation. She always showed great interest in this part of the African continent, where she maintained both overt and covert relations. If she had been able to conquer North Africa the threat to the south would have become very direct and real.

Thus the old routes of the world reveal a singular permanency and men tend to pass once again where they formerly passed.

I have always imagined a posthumous dialogue between Vasco da Gama and Ferdinand de Lesseps. Which of the two would have the last word? When Renan welcomed de Lesseps into the Académie Française on April 23, 1885, he addressed prophetic words to its newest member, words which were, to tell the truth, strangely disturbing by their profundity and their pessimism: 'Those great words: "I came not to bring peace but a sword" must often have been present in your mind. Once cut the isthmus becomes a passage, that is to say, a field of battle. Up to the present, one Bosphorus has sufficed to trouble the world. Now you have created a second more important than the first, because it does not merely join up two interior seas, but serves as a corridor of communications for all the great seas of the world. In the event of naval warfare it would prove the supreme interest, the point the whole world would fight to occupy as speedily as possible. You will thus have marked out the place for the great battles of the future.'

Transferring the sense of these impressive lines can we congratulate the Union of South Africa on finding itself, so to speak, astride one of the great maritime routes of the world? One of our wise old rural saws suggests that 'rivers and main roads make bad neighbours'.

# CHAPTER XVIII

# BASUTOLAND

BASUTOLAND, inhabited by the coloured tribe of Basutos, is British territory of approximately the same extent as Switzerland, and forms an enclave in South African territory. Administratively it is a Crown Colony under the Colonial Office in London, but, in fact, it is more a Protectorate administered in the spirit of a mandate. The contrast with South Africa, which surrounds it, is striking.

Basutoland is a mountainous country in which the Basutos once defended themselves against the Zulus in the east and the Boers in the west, who were making their way to the north in the Great Trek towards the middle of the last century. In the end the Basutos succeeded in preserving their individuality only by appealing for the protection of the British Crown (1868). Thus Great Britain exercises a sort of mandate and is under an obligation to respect the property, the customs and the institutions of her protégés. This situation derives from the agreement made with the Basuto chief Moshesh, a remarkable politician. The British Government would not lend itself to an annexation by the Union of South Africa unless the Basuto people agreed to it.

When the British Protectorate was instituted the Basutos had already come under Western influence. A French Protestant Mission, the Société Protestante des Missions de Paris, had been sending missionaries into the country since 1883, and the names of Coillard,

Casalis, Mabille, Arbousset and Pélissier are well known in French Protestant circles.

These pioneers, originally invited into the country by Moshesh himself, established Christian stations which still exist today, gathering the native elements they won for the Christian faith around the church, the school and sometimes the dispensary. The population is pastoral and patriarchal and has many biblical traits, which no doubt explains the success of those early missionaries. The meeting of Jesus and the Samaritan, the love story of Jacob and Rachel, and even the sacrifice of Isaac, are poetical stories which do not appear in the least out of place in a country where time seems to have moved more slowly than elsewhere. The biblical names given by the first missionaries to their stations, Cana, Bethany, Morija and so on, do not jar.

There is one part of France which can give us some idea of Basutoland, and that is the Causses de l'Aveyron, and do we not, in fact, always say that there is something a little African about it? Under a blue sky whose clarity in summer is never overcast, the light is both bright and yet very soft. Everything is dry, very dry, it does not rain for several months; everything is a tawny colour, and the high rocks which overhang the valleys and the uplands vibrate in the sun. The rare rivers flowing between abrupt banks along courses hollowed in the ground by erosion, contain only very little water moving slowly over banks of fine sand. But as soon as there is a little humidity, exquisite and delicate young foliage appears: willows of fresh green in the southern spring, giant eucalyptus, tall poplars, massive cypresses.

Chains of far-distant, almost unreal, mountains form the horizon, but there are rocky mounds everywhere, often with very steep sides, and at their feet lie sprawled the Basuto villages. The huts, which are at some distance from each other, are built either of clay or stone, sometimes cubical in shape, but generally cylindrical, and of an ochreous or chocolate colour with thatched roofs. In spring hedges of green aloes and peach trees in full blossom, all rosy, make these villages a charming sight.

Recalling the sordid suburbs of the mining cities it is difficult to imagine what makes the natives ever consent to leave these agreeable bucolic surroundings for the dreary urban life of our times.

The population is quite dense and one gets the impression that the inhabitants live less on their fields of maize than on their many flocks, which still belong to them and which graze on soil which has remained their property. That is the great difference between Basutoland and South Africa.

Here in Basutoland the native has retained his soul, living his own independent life under his traditional chiefs and, above all, with his own means of existence. In the spirit of the Protectorate the British administration recognizes the chiefs and relies on them to a certain extent without seeking to further the evolution of this archaic society so that the impression is created of a sort of National Park in which the way of life lived a century ago is preserved. Up till now the outlook of the Protectorate and that of the missionaries has derived on the whole from the same inspiration, which is that of preservation.

There are two separate missions working side by

side, the Protestant Mission, which is primarily French and has thirty-eight parishes, and the Catholic Mission of lay brothers, formerly French but now chiefly French Canadian, with forty-three parishes.

The earliest French Protestant missionaries were not content merely to evangelize, they strove also to instruct. At present, like the Catholics, they are striving to preserve the artisan character of their technical training in order that this Basuto society, which, though still primitive is not savage, shall continue to retain its pre-industrial character. However, it would seem that the British administration is now beginning to train technicians for large-scale industry, and it is encouraged in this direction by the demands of the natives themselves. But one is inclined to ask oneself whether it is not a mistake, particularly when one knows that such trainees cannot be usefully placed in Basutoland, which has no industry at all, or in the Union of South Africa, where the colour bar is supreme.

When the first French Protestant missionaries arrived in Basutoland the total population was 30,000 at the outside. However, the progress of hygiene, the establishment of law and order, and the abolition of wars and massacres have had the same effects here as elsewhere, and it is now estimated that the population amounts to 600,000, which is an excessive figure because the country is not in a position to feed them all. On the whole it is a poor country, and, into the bargain, the soil is threatened by erosion. The climate is dry, but the country is subject to sudden and violent storms when the rain pours down in torrents, and in running away it hollows out deep gulleys which become deeper and deeper after each such storm. In addition, too many animals are being raised on the land; deprived of grass, what remains of the top-soil is blown away by gusts of wind leaving the bare and infertile rock.

A campaign against soil erosion has now begun, but it may already be too late. What else can be done to feed these people, whose numbers are still increasing, To industrialize the country would mean to open the door to all the problems which worry the outside world. To prospect for mines — and there are undoubtedly deposits in Basutoland — would mean to set up the golden calf.

In existing circumstances the surplus population just emigrates, attracted to the compounds of Johannesburg and the factories in the big towns. There are many Basutos in the lowest quarters there, uprooted and demoralized men who, returning to visit their native villages, help to contaminate those who have stayed behind. The original patriarchal nature of the country is now gradually changing but there are still some curious survivals.

In accordance with its mission as guardian and protector, and whilst respecting the principle that the power of the local chiefs and headmen should remain, the administration has found itself compelled to limit their powers because some of these chiefs are the exploiters of their people. It would seem that a latent revolt against Christianity and the spirit it represents is crystallizing around these chiefs.

The power of 'magic' in primitive societies is well known, and recently there has been a recrudescence of paganism combined with a renewal of 'magic' practices, which has led to a disturbing reappearance of ritual crimes. These crimes have been committed, or at least inspired, not by the more backward and primitive natives, but, in particular, by natives who occupy the position of chiefs, men who have been brought up as Christians, and who, in some cases, even hold university degrees. In the towns, too, the authorities are disturbed by the increasing frequency of crimes such as robbery, rape and murder. A crisis has, in fact, arisen and long years of Christian educational work are now being put to a severe test.

The attitude adopted by the administration towards the native question in this quite exceptional territory seems to be the best possible in the circumstances, namely to preserve the traditional tribal status of the people and to keep them completely apart from white men, who are forbidden to settle in the territory.

This system has succeeded because it has left the natives their lands, and that is just what the Union of South Africa has not done, and it would find itself very much at a loss to support its 8,000,000 natives on the land reserves it has so parsimoniously accorded to them.

A protectorate seems the best solution for coloured peoples at this stage of development. But peoples, like children, finally grow up no matter who they are; at least, they become adult in age if not in mind. And it is impossible to prevent their growth.

# CHAPTER XIX

# WITHOUT GOLD SOUTH AFRICA WOULD BE A VERY ORDINARY COUNTRY

THE odd impression made by the economy of South Africa is that of a poor man — or, shall we say perhaps a man in modest circumstances whose material resources and talents are both moderate — who has suddenly won first prize in a lottery. Without the discovery of gold in 1886, and, of less importance, the discovery of diamonds in 1870, South Africa would in all probability have remained a pastoral country not particularly attractive to immigrants. How many now live in South Africa who would not be there but for these discoveries!

Although the country is large in area — approximately three times the size of France — its soil, as has been stated, is poor, and the area suitable for agriculture is restricted, representing no more that 15 per cent of the whole. Travelling through these immense spaces one is struck by their dryness, often even their absolute aridity. It is in reality a stock-raising country where sheep and cattle are everything. The sheep yield a fine wool just because they are not particularly well fed. There are certainly some very fine outlying districts, for instance in Cape Province and Natal, where fruit, vines and the sugar-cane grow well, but the typical South African is the Boer, living on the plains with his cattle and sheep.

The special conditions of these regions have made him into a sheep and cattle breeder and not a farmer. On those wide spaces, where limits are non-existent, there is so much free land; the Boer is accustomed to extensive breeding, and what he grows in the way of maize or wheat represents only an almost negligible supplement. The result is that no care is given to the soil; when one area is exhausted, the Boer simply moves on to the next. The cattle and sheep themselves also receive very little attention and they are let loose to feed themselves as best they can. And if there is any work to be done it is left to the native to do it.

These Boers are called farmers, like our agriculturists in Europe, but there the resemblance ceases. Age-old experience has taught us that soil is something that can be kept in good heart only by ceaseless labour. After generations of neglect South Africa is now beginning to learn this lesson. The native in his reserve has not been any more far-sighted. The threat of erosion is made all the graver by the fact that two-thirds of the population live from the land, even though agriculture represents only about 10 per cent of the national revenues.

This disproportion is explained if we remember that out of the total population of 11,392,000 the Whites represent only 20 per cent against the natives' 68 per cent. In the distribution of the national income the lion's share goes to the 2,373,000 'Europeans', and that is why the country creates an impression — a paradoxical impression incidentally — of wealth. The white population of South Africa do, in fact, enjoy a high standard of living compared with average standards in Europe.

It is the presence of gold which has raised South Africa from the modest economic circumstances which would otherwise have been her normal destiny. Quite suddenly a first-class mining industry of great vigour and of ultra-modern inspiration sprang up in what had been the solitude of the Veldt. Its gold is the main source of the prosperity of the country as a whole. Gold (which must be considered a commodity like any other) represents 60 per cent of the total exports of the country. The mines accounted for 23 per cent of the revenues of the State in 1939 and 16 per cent in 1944. The Witwatersrand mines employ 41,000 'Europeans' and 318,000 natives, not counting the labour force employed by all the subsidiary industries grouped around the production of gold.

If the production of gold were to cease the ensuing crisis would be disastrous. Happily for South Africa the supposition is baseless, because a new strike has been made only recently in the Orange Free State to replace the mines of the Transvaal should they ever become exhausted. But even mining resources cannot be inexhaustible. Without gold South Africa would be a very ordinary country — certainly not destitute, but less blessed than Canada or the Argentine.

The situation has not escaped the attention of South African governments, which, since the first world war at least, have considered the question of a substitute for gold in the form of industrial development. There are a number of factors favourable to this idea: for one thing there is an abundant supply of coal in the Transvaal and in Natal at low prices (the annual production is now 25,000,000 tons); in addition there are important deposits of iron ore and manganese, and, of course, there are good supplies of raw wool and skins.

On the other hand, however, the labour power of white workers is very dear whilst that of natives is of low productivity. But the greatest difficulty is represented by the narrow limits of the local market: only the 2,000,000 Whites have real purchasing power.

Interesting problems rise in this connection. It would be to the advantage of industry to develop the purchasing power of the natives and the half-breeds by employing them at good wages not merely as labourers, but as skilled and semi-skilled workers. But any such policy would meet with the implacable opposition of the trade unions, which defend the privileges of their white members and seek to exclude coloured workers from all skilled occupations. Up to the present their opposition has been decisive. Now the interests of the mining industry are different again. The mines require large quantities of cheap labour, and they can recruit it, at least at the lower levels, only amongst the native population. If industrial wages caused mining wages to rise, many mines whose profit margin has narrowed owing to the gradual exhaustion of their deposits would have to close down.

To tell the truth, the problem does not arise in such a clear-cut-fashion because first of all industry finds a market in the mines and secondly the mines themselves control numerous local industries. Owing to this fact, and in particular to the war, mining and industrial developments have been able to go hand in hand. Factories are being built everywhere, not only in Johannesburg or Pretoria, but also in Durban, Port Elizabeth and Capetown. Thanks to the general

C H

## SOUTH A
## BRITISH (

T H E accession
Afrikander rais
between the U
British Commonweal
developing rapidly,
made almost more q
The British Empire is
its strength today lie
inexhaustible capacity
tions; like the reed in t
break.

According to Profess
has already experienc
first British Empire w
and died of it with
colonies. The second,
settlement colonies, su
without difficulty, whe
cal maturity did not fa
as so many people h
wrought by Liberalisn
third empire, based on
their complete indeper
separated themselves f
have remained free mer
equality with the mothe
I believe that a fourth

shortage it is easy to find a market for their products. Machinery is being imported on a big scale and prosperity reigns.

The crisis will arise when South African industrial production reaches the limits of local purchasing power, because then it will become necessary to export the unsaleable domestic surplus. That will prove possible and profitable only if the costs of production are low enough to enable South Africa to compete successfully on the world markets. But nowadays all countries are industrializing themselves and seeking to export their goods. Manufactured goods represented only 18.8 per cent of South Africa's exports in 1946, but 78.5 per cent of her imports, a relation which emphasizes the still undeveloped economic character of the country.

The fact is that South Africa still needs to import manufactured goods and capital. At one time Great Britain traditionally provided both the one and the other, but since the war first place has been taken by the United States. South Africa has bought so much from her that she is now, like all other countries, short of dollars, and her trade balance has become disturbingly passive. In 1946 the value of imports rose to 214,000,000 pounds sterling, whilst the value of exports was only 196,000,000, of which 108,000,000 pounds were represented by gold, a circumstance which gives us some idea of the important role played by the fabulous yellow metal in the economy of the country.

Despite U.S. progress, Great Britain's position is still strong. The gold-mining industry of the Transvaal remains attached to London by a thousand subtle

threads: throug[
experts for one t[
tion and traini[
another, who, ev[
tans, maintain c[
it is attached to[
tion. In this re[
should we say, n[
is here that we c[
of that traditiona[
tary but also con[
zone.

In the end we[
and we might we[
would be able t[
without the assis[
worth of gold wh[
able to export ev[
The transition fr[
an economy foun[
revolution. The [
good fortune, hav[
lottery ticket, wou[
of life and have to[
economic climate.[

formation, one in which the Dominion conception and Dominion relations to the Commonwealth will once again change profoundly. In the original conception of the term a Dominion was a colony of British settlers who, arriving at political maturity, thereby achieved independence without seceding from the family. The fact that they were members of the family in the first place was essential. This was the case with both Australia and New Zealand, whose populations are homogeneous in this important respect. It must be admitted that the conception is not so essentially reasonable when a Dominion includes elements which are not of British origin. In Canada, for instance, 30 per cent of the population is French; nevertheless the system still does not function too badly. However, in the Union of South Africa the Afrikander represent 60 per cent of the white population, and as one can hardly expect the vanquished in a war which lies only half a century back in history to be loyally devoted to their conqueror, the Dominion conception there can obviously not be the same as in Australasia.

The difficulty becomes even greater when the Dominion idea is extended to countries whose inhabitants, like India for example, are not even members of the white race and have no reason whatever, either of sentiment or political communion, to remain attached to the British Empire. To give them independence means that instead of desiring to remain within the old community they will naturally be tempted to leave it. According to the classic formula, the ripe fruit falls from the tree, but the severance is for good and all. To extend the Dominion conception to such countries is illogical and unreasonable; at least it is if the aim is to gain the same advantages as have resulted by granting the same concession to real members of the family. Incidentally, Great Britain has already had some experience in this respect: Ireland, a hostile Dominion, has proclaimed herself a Republic. The King of England has never been able to go there in recent times, and the country took no part in the recent war.

Thus if such countries are to be kept within the Commonwealth nevertheless, something like a new constitution will have to be devised to enable them to remain, and it is for this reason that a fourth British Empire is essential if Dominion status is to be extended to countries whose loyalty to the Crown cannot be based on sentiment. This applies not only with regard to Eire, but also to India and, to a great extent, to the Union of South Africa.

A member of the Chatham House group has proposed a formula known as 'External Association' to meet the case. It is designed to permit such colonies, or former colonies, which, whilst not being members of the family or desiring to become so, may nevertheless desire to remain within the Commonwealth (for instance, for economic or security reasons, or because they need the support of a big power like the British Empire in their foreign policy) to do so.

It is perhaps Eire which offers us the best example of what can be done in this respect. The Irish, we know, do not love England. They claim independence, and not a friendly independence at that. They are republican and the Crown is nothing to them. However, the geographical position of their country and the fact that their exports are almost entirely imported by

Great Britain, links their fate to that of the sister island. And thus we are presented with the paradox of a republic which has a king. Eire is a member of the Commonwealth; whilst recognizing no solidarity with the rest of its members, she nevertheless makes no attempt to leave it. Negotiations are now in progress between Dublin and London which may well result in an accord, and that would be a new masterpiece of British Empire policy.

We should consider the position of the Union of South Africa in the British Commonwealth in much the same fashion. The memory of the Boer War has not been eradicated and the Afrikander do not like the English. During the late war some of them rejoiced at Britain's difficulties. Some of them have even been attracted by Nazidom and its racial intransigence. Does this mean that the new government of the Union will lead it out of the Empire? Not at all, because a country like the Union of South Africa cannot live alone in the neighbourhood of an over-populated Asia whose people are rapidly awakening. In addition it is not in a position to think of either economic or financial independence, and here its traditional bonds with Great Britain make themselves felt: it was Great Britain which developed the country and built up its mining, technical and financial structure. The attraction of the dollar may be strong, but nevertheless subtle bonds attach the country to sterling. No doubt the wild slogans of the extreme nationalists give vent to deep-seated feelings, but the responsible government of the country cannot shape its policy in accordance with them. When it governs it has always to remember that its majority is very narrow, that two-fifths of the white population are British by origin, and that a noteworthy minority of Afrikander are moderates and opposed to all excesses.

Thus the Union of South Africa will remain within the Commonwealth, but with a government like Dr. Malan's in power Great Britain can no longer count on those relations of confidence which existed when Field Marshal Smuts was at the helm. The Governor-General of South Africa, the representative of the King, is an Afrikander, chosen, in fact, not by the King but by the Government of South Africa. The official bond between London and Pretoria has been reduced to the person of the British High Commissioner.

It is in this sense that we must envisage the principle of 'External Association', though without overlooking the fact that excellent results can be obtained from its application, precisely because the system is not asked to do more than it is in a position to do: no sentiment where there is no room for sentiment, but an association based on reason, or, better still, on necessity. Since the Statute of Westminster the South African Union has secured everything in the way of independence that an independent State itself could ask, but nowadays real independence is permitted only to a very few countries properly called imperial.

In the fourth British Empire the great Dominions of British origin, such as Australia, New Zealand and Canada, are tending towards a friendly independence which is becoming more and more *de facto* independence. In such cases the term Dominion is no longer suitable and it is therefore falling more and more into disuse. Great Britain herself has become more European as a result of the recent war, and at the same time she is also becoming more 'colonial' in the narrower sense of the term. She seems to be concentrating her interest on the new African Empire she is building up in Kenya, Tanganyika, Nyasaland and Rhodesia, an Empire which is strictly colonial and not Commonwealth. She is, so to speak, at home there in her own right as Great Britain. The third category of relations is expressed in the term 'External Association', which we have attempted to explain above.

The British political genius is capable, I both believe and hope, of performing once again the miracle of proving that the illogical can nevertheless survive.

# CHAPTER XXI

# AT THE TOMB OF CECIL RHODES

ABOUT twenty miles to the south of Bulawayo rises the chain of the Matopo Hills. It was there in a wild part of the country that Cecil Rhodes desired to be buried. He discovered the spot at the time of the Matabele revolt in 1896. Their great chief Lobengula, whose name will remain alive in history, had been defeated in 1893. The town of Bulawayo was founded on the very spot where his Kraal had stood, and in the garden of the present Residence one can still see the very tree under which he held his court. Then the Matabele revolted, and the memory of their revolt is still alive amongst the older residents. Finally Cecil Rhodes, whose prestige amongst the natives was very great, proposed a meeting in the heart of the Matopo Hills to negotiate peace. Together with five unarmed companions he proceeded to the agreed rendezvous. The risk was considerable, but the authority of the Great White Chief was immense, and after a long palaver a peace was concluded which has lasted down to the present day: no longer with Lobengula, dead and buried in a mysterious spot, but with his lieutenants.

In 1896 Rhodes, who was then forty-three years old, knew that his days were numbered. He was to die in 1902. The vigorous and magnificently creative rhythm of his life was due to that feeling of urgency which spurred him on in his immense projects. 'So much to do; so little done,' he once sadly observed.

At the time of the Matabele revolt he was once on horseback in the mysterious depths of the Matopo Hills when he came across a scene which captivated and amazed him by its grand beauty. In the centre of it was an isolated rocky summit as though made to draw the eye: 'One view of the world,' he said. It was there that he desired his remains to lie.

From Bulawayo the route passes through countryside which is typical of that enormous and unknown continent: widely spaced trees in gnarled exotic forms, grass and herbage reduced at the end of the dry season to a sort of matting underfoot, and a fierce sun whose glare drains away all colour. Mountains rear up in an undisciplined mass with no design comprehensible to the eye of the beholder. A granite eruption has flung up great mounds where the rock, washed and polished by the rains, resembles the spine of some great elephant or hippopotamus; enormous rounded boulders lie side by side and one on top of the other.

It was one of those mounds in the middle of a vast arena that Rhodes indicated as his last resting place. The Matabele, who knew the place, called it Malindidzimu, seat of benevolent spirits. The great South African desired to make it — the expression is his own — the pantheon of those who had merited well of their country. The way was so steep that when he died his coffin, placed in an artillery waggon, could be dragged there only by a team of twelve oxen. The spot is truly exceptional: a bare granite ridge ochreous in colour, its sides flecked with yellow patches, and on the summit five or six massive rocks like great balls. It is between these boulders that Rhodes's tomb lies in simple grandeur. A rectangular slab of stone with a bronze plaque and the inscription: 'Here lie the remains of Cecil John Rhodes.' That is all.

It is a sign of modesty when a man causes all his titles to be printed on his visiting card; the proud man puts just his name, and that is enough. Rhodes has had nothing inscribed on his grave beyond his name; neither the date of his birth nor that of his death; and none of his distinctions, famous though they were: Prime Minister of Cape Colony, President of De Beers, the Rand Mines, the British South Africa Company, and so on. To what purpose? The name is enough. Pride in great men does not shock us.

It is truly a spot destined for a monument in the etymological sense of the term, that is to say, a place proper for reflection, proper for the edification of man. It is reported that on his first sight of the spot an American journalist exclaimed: 'Gee! What a place for a Coca-Cola sign!' For myself I prefer the expression of Barrès: 'A place of deep significance for the soul of man.'

But is it the soul we should speak of here? I would rather think of it as a unique place of energy, vision and political creation. Many people, even in South Africa — but not in Rhodesia — regard Rhodes as having been primarily a business man. No doubt the great gold and diamond magnate was that too, but he was also something else, something very different. The genius and originality of this great builder of empire lie precisely in the fact that for him business, politics, conquest and his imperial mission were all nothing but different facets of the same aim whose pursuit had its origin in an inspiration fundamentally mystical.

Most countries tend in a certain direction; in

principle the trend is geographic but in reality it is charged with idealism, imagination and poetry on account of the promise it holds: for the United States it was 'the West', for Hitler it was 'the East', for our North Africans it is 'the South'. For Rhodes it was 'the North', 'My North' as he called it, the direction of the Cape to Cairo route. Symbolically all his statues face in that direction.

In the life of Rhodes there was one drama which contradicted his whole political conception: the Jameson Raid. The greatness of the man lay in the fact that his ideas were always constructive. If he had an enemy he invariably sought to win the man over to his side, and in order to do that he first sought to understand him. That is what he did with Barnato, his rival in Kimberley, and with Hofmeyr, the Dutch-speaking South African with whom he founded a new South-African patriotism. And without doubt that is what he would have done with Oom Kruger had not some wicked fairy laid a nugget of gold in the cradle of the Transvaal. And thus the Devil took a hand in the game. Rhodes did not himself order the execution of the Jameson Raid, the incident which finally led to war, but he allowed it to be prepared. It was a flaw in a great career, but fundamentally the incentive was not greed for gold, but the drive towards the North.

That was why he desired that his tomb should be on that world route in the Matopo Hills rather than in Capetown where he spent most of his time. The site of the monument set up to him in the Cape is perhaps more beautiful, with a Mediterranean romanticism almost Athenian. But that at Bulawayo is the more significant. And it is in Rhodesia that his statues best represent him to us. People who knew him have described him to me: a full face with a pointed chin conveying an impression of strength perhaps a trifle stolid; the very clear blue eyes of a man of vision, a man who took thought for the future; a small mouth with fine lips; the voice rather weak and a little uneven. The entire lower part of the face seemed to express a will of iron, an obstinacy which would break all those who opposed his projects. The man is very near. I would have recognized him. And yet he has already entered into legend. Henri de Regnier speaks of landscapes *fabuleusement anonymes*. African landscapes are often like that, but Rhodes did much to give them the memory of a tremendous presence.

# CHAPTER XXII

# LINES OF DEMARCATION

BEFORE the Civil War came to settle the issue, a line of demarcation ran across the United States dividing those States in which slavery was still tolerated from those in which it had been abolished. It was the famous Mason-Dixon Line. Making all proper allowances, and although slavery has, of course, been abolished, a similar sort of line still exists in Africa. To the south of it a white settlement colony regards the maintenance and defence of its position as the essential aim of its policy, whilst to the north a colony of exploitation has come to consider itself under an obligation to protect the coloured people against the often excessive pretentions of European immigrants. In view of the outlook and attitude such a line implies its existence is obviously of fundamental importance; confining ourselves deliberately to South and East Africa let us therefore try to discover just where it runs. The Union of South Africa represents the one pole of colonization, whilst Kenya represents the other; but where is the line to be drawn?

We are faced here with two different conceptions. Communities of the white race, sufficiently strong in numbers to aspire to an independent existence, regard their defence and that of the civilization they represent against absorption by a numerically stronger community of colour as their predominant aim, as their sacred mission. The 'White Africa' formula (like that of 'White Australia') then takes the form of a dogma beyond all discussion, with its roots in feeling rather than reason. It is, in fact, a question of life or death for a white community surrounded by a coloured population ten, even twenty, times as numerous. The Union of South Africa and Southern Rhodesia, with 2,300,000 and 105,000 Whites respectively against 8,000,000 and 1,800,000 natives respectively, belong in this category. The rights of the natives, no matter what may be the attitude towards them, are never in any circumstances regarded as taking precedence over the interests of the European community, which in its own view, is established there as a permanency to found a people and to constitute an outpost of the white race in the world. As soon as such groups become autonomous collectives they naturally tend to demand political independence, and experience has taught Great Britain that it is wise to accede to their demands. It is in this fashion that Southern Rhodesia is developing towards the status of a Dominion, and that the Union of South Africa has already arrived at full factual independence.

On the other hand, in what we have termed colonies of exploitation the Whites are present only in very small numbers and they do not constitute what one could justly call a community or society in the same sense. They consist simply of an élite of administrators and leaders, some of whom have certainly come without any intention of returning, but most of whom will finally return to their homes in Europe. In such circumstances the native never appears as a competitor potentially capable of taking the place of the white worker, because there are no white workers in this sense; the native is a labourer whom it seems wise, both for economic and for humanitarian reasons, to treat with consideration. This view was certainly not adopted from the very beginning, but gradually established itself, and finally found expression in the mandatory form, the European considering himself henceforth as the teacher and protector of the native.

That at least is the position to which the Colonial Office has come in practice even though it is not formally under any such an obligation by a mandate from the League of Nations or the United Nations Organization. An official declaration made in 1923 on the subject of Kenya specified that the interests of the natives should be considered paramount over those of the immigrated farmers whenever the two might come into conflict.

A later definition made in 1931 and confirmed recently (in 1948), laid it down that the interests of the natives, whilst not necessarily having paramountcy over those of the immigrant farmers, should not be sacrificed to them, and that Whites and natives should be considered as partners in the country. In such circumstances it is clearly necessary that the ultimate control of native policy should be in the hands of the colonial administration, and this excludes the possibility of Dominion Status. One can now observe the political significance of the difference between these two types of colonial society, the one tending towards independence and the other necessarily remaining under the authority of the home country.

And, in fact, we should harbour no illusions: to turn a colony into a Dominion means to hand over the native to the mercies of the settler, that is to say, to withdraw the protecting hand of a metropolitan colonial administration, more liberal because it is further away and less directly interested. In Kenya the native is protected; in the Union of South Africa he is not. Logically therefore we are bound to conclude that if Great Britain really regards herself as the protector of the native she cannot desire the formation of any new Dominions in Central Africa. The contrast we have been discussing arises in such a fashion between Southern and Northern Rhodesia that there is little doubt that our African Mason-Dixon Line runs between these two colonies.

In Southern Rhodesia the existing regime is that of a Dominion, though with certain limitations. For instance, any legislation affecting the interests of the natives requires the approval of the Colonial Office, which, through the mediation of the Governor, thus exercises the equivalent of a veto. However, development is proceeding towards the stage of full autonomy, which is apparently near. Southern Rhodesia is very British, although a form of Rhodesian patriotism certainly exists, but the ideas of the white farmer about the natives hardly differ from those current in South Africa, so that in the last resort Southern Rhodesians and South Africans find themselves on the same side of the fence: they are white communities on the defensive, and the natives are granted representative rights only in a very grudging and limited fashion. If the farmers did not see to it, the white trade unions — the real symbols of privilege and reaction in this part of the world — certainly would.

The situation in Northern Rhodesia, where there are 1,500,000 natives and only 27,000 Whites, is more complicated. Many of these Whites are miners of the Copper Belt, and their attitude towards the native labourers is very similar to that of the 'European' miners in the Transvaal. They are quite determined to maintain a colour bar which makes skilled employment the exclusive privilege of the White. On the other hand the British colonial administration regards itself as called upon to protect the native. In the case of Basutoland, and also of one or two local chiefs, it exercises a protectorate by virtue of actual protective treaties concluded with the native tribes. In these circumstances the regime tends towards autonomy but never arrives at it. The Legislative Council of the colony is a small parliament of twenty-three members, nine of whom are directly nominated by the Governor. The fourteen others are elected, ten by the Whites and four (directly or indirectly) by the natives themselves. A new departure is that of these latter four, two must actually be natives. In all questions relating to native policy the Governor can always be certain of a reliable majority, consisting of the nine members he appoints directly, and the four who represent the natives.

The presence of two natives in this assembly has not failed to stir white public opinion not only in Rhodesia, but also in South Africa. It does, in fact, introduce a principle which the intransigent elements of the 'European defence movement' regard as dangerous. Incidentally it places Northern Rhodesia in the same category as Kenya and the other British colonies of East Africa which are administered in a mandatory spirit. There is much talk of a Central African Dominion to include the two Rhodesias and Nyasaland. I have difficulty in believing in the practicability of the project except in the form of a rather vague federation, and it is likely that the British Government does not regard the idea with any favour.

We have previously suggested that the traditional Dominion conception is applicable only with regard to exclusively British settlement colonies. But where the Whites, even if they are British, represent only a minority surrounded by a majority of natives, then to grant them Dominion Status would mean virtually to abandon the natives and to leave them without proper protection. And if the vote were given to the natives the logical result would be the inevitable elimination of the Whites. Thus some form of administrative tutelage is essential, at least until a solution has been found which will preserve both white civilization and the rights of the natives. In our own colonies we have approached these grave problems from a different angle, but in that part of Africa through which I have just travelled it would seem that the ethnic and political topography is shaping its outlook and attitude and drawing its lines of demarcation in the way I have described.

# CHAPTER XXIII

## SOUTH AFRICAN CONCLUSIONS

SOUTH AFRICA with her glistening gold and diamonds stirs our imagination with thoughts of luxury and riches. In reality, as we have seen, her soil is poor, and her population sparse and incapable of feeding itself adequately.

To repeat: the country owes its riches, or what serves it in place of riches, to the yellow metal which suddenly caused an immense mining camp to spring up with all the spendthrift atmosphere which gold invariably brings in its train. And further it owes a singular ease of life to the fact that slavery prevailed there for a long time, and still survives in an attenuated fashion in the form of serfdom embracing the whole native population: from the richest to the poorest, all Whites in South Africa have acquired the habit of letting themselves be waited upon. And finally we can number amongst the causes of South Africa's prosperity the fact that she is situated on one of the great world maritime routes far removed (up to the present) from the area of modern battle. When Ferdinand de Lesseps opened the Suez Canal in 1869 the old route round the Cape found itself relegated into semi-obscurity, but the diamonds of Kimberley (1870) and the gold of Johannesburg (1886), and finally the decline in the usefulness of the Mediterranean as a maritime route in time of war, once again put South Africa into the international limelight.

Some of these prosperity factors are truly outstanding, and it is not for nothing that South African shares enjoy the greatest consideration on the Stock Exchanges of the world. Nevertheless we should not overlook one or two disturbing signs even though they refer to a still somewhat distant future. Must we say, to adapt a phrase of Aynard concerning Deschanel, that the country has a great future behind it? No, I don't think we need go as far as that, but we are perhaps entitled to doubt whether South Africa is still a young country. And the directly interested parties feel misgivings — they make no attempt to conceal it — about their own future.

Let us not attach too much importance to the hostility of the Boers and the British. They are two sections of the white race, and in defence of their common civilization they will sooner or later be obliged to act in concert. 'White Africa' is more important than either flag or language in that dangerously subsiding outpost of Western civilization. It is threatened ethnically from without and stealthily undermined from within by the subtle menace of degeneration.

There is no doubt whatever that the disdain in which a whole series of manual tasks are held there must be regarded as a sign of degeneration. In a society which has known slavery and which, like the Southern States of the U.S.A., still retains certain domestic habits of the period, there are a great many things, including very simple ones, that 'are not done' by Whites. Such tasks are 'Kaffir's work', good for niggers. One can still meet with the atmosphere of the old 'plantations', and it is here that the 'Poor White' came into being as a deplorable example of physical and moral degeneration. And let us harbour no illusions in this respect. Although the number of these social wrecks has considerably diminished in recent years it has come about only because they have been arbitrarily protected against native competition and systematically provided with employment in which they do not justify their keep. In a society in which white and coloured men worked freely side by side the latter would naturally and logically be preferred for more primitive forms of employment; but not all Whites show superior ability and the result is therefore that in the lower reaches they would be condemned to unemployment and pauperism. They can be sustained by racial solidarity certainly, but they represent a dead weight on society.

Not only are certain human elements in Africa threatened with degeneration, but the soil is too, and for the same reason. Things have been taken too easily. The native is a nomad who exhausts the soil — and then goes on to the next stretch, a proceeding which can be continued only as long as there is still free land available. And the Boer farmer himself has grown up in a tradition which is hardly much different: the traditions of the Great Trek have strengthened his nomad mentality. He lets his herds and flocks roam through the immensity of the Veldt, and he does little more than scratch the soil to maintain his own farm; and then he, too, goes on without bothering his head about the maintenance or reconstitution of a soil threatened with erosion.

Generally speaking the soil of South Africa is poor, and now it is exhausted in addition. What is needed is a policy of systematic irrigation to conserve the water which is so rare, a collective policy to defend the soil and preserve it against the depredations of the storms. But the financial magnitude of such a task would be enormous, not to speak of the labour required. And nothing has made such a population suited for the kind of work our peasants do; even the immigrants now flocking into the country from Great Britain are not the pioneering types of former days. They are full of pretentions concerning their standard of living and they are anxious to reap before they have sown. Solid and hard-working Mediterranean folk are what is required there, but, as we know, Anglo-Saxons despise 'Wogs'.

It is fortunate for South Africa that there is still gold in her soil and that new deposits have recently been discovered in the Orange Free State. There is also coal and iron in sufficient quantities to form a solid double basis for heavy industry. And then there is wool and sugar-cane and the Mediterranean fruits of the Cape. But without the gold all that would hardly make South Africa more than a second-rate country. Adventurers would not have gone there, or speculators, or investors of capital. Her civilization would have remained pastoral, easy going, peaceable and without history.

But with Kimberley and Johannesburg, South Africa, for good or evil, has become a part of world history. And with the renewed importance of the Cape route, the successor of the Suez Canal route in the event of war, her role has become even more important, particularly as the southern hemisphere tends to become a refuge not only for men but also for man's industries. In consequence a tide which seemed to be receding now shows signs of rising again. But let us not deceive ourselves, with her gold South Africa is certainly in the limelight; without it she would be a very ordinary country with poor soil and no particular asset in the character of its population — definitely inferior to either Canada or the Argentine.

What sort of a future has South Africa in these circumstances? 2,000,000 Whites against 8,000,000 natives represents a disturbing proportion and creates only a very narrow economic basis. The native is developing rapidly and there is very little hope of an improvement in the relative numerical strength of the white population. And incidentally, seeing that the native is indispensable, South Africa does not know whether to hope for his increase or to fear it. Further, even at present his 'reserves' are hardly sufficient to maintain him. This country, self-styled 'new', is already compelled to import a part of its foodstuffs.

The natives are increasing in numbers in the towns, where they are losing their own traditions without acquiring the more favourable aspects of ours. The colour bar systematically confines them to inferior employment and every obstacle is placed in the way of their advancement.

Fear is at the bottom of this policy, and no effective solution whatever suggests itself. If the policy of 'keeping the nigger in his place' is continued there will one day be a revolt either in the form of a general strike which will bring everything to a standstill or in the form of a new revolt of Spartakus led by the coloured syndicalist leaders, half witch doctors, half prophets, but encouraged and armed by Moscow. On the other hand, if they are allowed to compete on equal terms with white workers then the lower reaches amongst these 'Europeans' will be reduced to unemployment and pauperism.

I believe, too, that there is another storm about to gather which should not be overlooked: the infiltration and competition of the Indian. The threat is tangible only in Durban, but there is now an Indian State. As long as Great Britain remains strong there is nothing to fear in this direction, but if South Africa stood alone is it likely that India would be prepared to put up for long with the discriminatory measures about which she now complains so bitterly?

World opinion is harsh towards South Africa, too harsh in my opinion. Not that I approve — and who could approve? — of the utterly uncharitable attitude of the South Africans towards the coloured people. But to the Americans who protest I am tempted to say: 'He that is without sin among you, let him cast the first stone,' and to Europeans I would say: 'You know nothing about the daily problem of colour.' The extenuating circumstance lies in the fact that these Whites represent an outpost of our race and our civilization which is being compelled to defend itself.

Let us be just: the country has produced some great figures, military, financial and political. I call men like Cecil Rhodes, Kruger, Botha and Smuts great. But how narrow the human basis of that Western outpost is! And how far off and isolated! I was deeply impressed by the pessimism of the South Africans with whom I talked. They could not say in exactly what fashion, but they felt that the future held a menace for them. A weak garrison in an ocean of colour, they were afraid of being submerged. If they asked me what I thought I should be tempted to reply: 'If you have no children then for the immediate future you have not much to fear. If you have a son, take care. And if you have grandchildren, who can say what their situation will be in fifty years time?'

# CHAPTER XXIV

## CAPE TO CAIRO

I HAVE now flown over the whole African continent from the Cape to Cairo. How does Africa
look to the traveller along that famous route? Let
us take a bird's-eye view of it.

At Capetown one might think oneself on the Basque
coast and over the vineyards of Provence. It is only
further to the north that Africa proper appears. But
over the desert-like steppes of the Great Karroo one
might at first think oneself in Mexico: it has the same
stony aridity and the same indefinite horizons, whilst
the conventional shapes of the cactus stand out above
the parched herbage. And then, after a transition
not easy to describe, the Veldt of the Orange Free
State and the Transvaal gradually appears, an endless stretch of vast treeless plains whose bare expanse
may well enthuse the lovers of wide open spaces. It is
easy to imagine the legendary and leisurely Boer
migrations of the past when one sees the traditional
waggon drawn by sixteen placid and powerful yoked
oxen still in use today. Sometimes their place is
taken by ten, twelve or fourteen mules. The ancient
rhythm of life still goes on here, belying the throbbing
tremendous activity of the hundred mines in Johannesburg.

Beyond the Limpopo, the northern frontier of the
Transvaal, a new region, a region more authentically
African, opens up, a sort of Savannah. One finds it
everywhere, in Rhodesia, in the Belgian Congo and

in Kenya, and everywhere it is the same: covered with vegetation, yellow in the dry season and green as soon as the rains come, it is an indefinite disorderly growth with smallish, gnarled and dishevelled trees, something like a neglected orchard, where wandering cattle browse on what they can find. There are no landmarks, but an oppressive monotony of sparse vegetation with here and there giant termite mounds on which not so long ago, I am told, lions would spring to look around for their prey. Wild elephants continue to flourish in Rhodesia; in the immediate neighbourhood of the Zambesi Falls, and even near palatial residences, they have recently become a peril for the over-confident globe-trotter, thinking to find in them the counterpart of the chamois of Tartarin, who, the day over and his work done, would retire to the enjoyment of a glass of mulled wine.

And then comes the great Lake of Tanganyika, a fissure in the earth's crust so deep that the bottom of the lake (almost 5000 feet in depth) is over 2000 feet below sea level. It was on its east bank that Stanley 'discovered' Livingstone, whom he greeted with the now famous laconic and most authentically British phrase: 'Dr. Livingstone, I presume?' That was in 1871. Since then the region has fallen back into its age-old anonymity, but it still retains all its exotic beauty and its majesty. A little further on we can even use the word charming — a most unusual term for Africa — to describe the scenery of Lake Kivu. Set in a mountainous region rich in cattle, whose grassy hills are always green, its winding shores studded with the elegant villas of Belgian colonists and its many creeks, promontories and small islands give it the appearance of an Italian lake. In the distance volcanoes whose cones are half collapsed have spread out vast wastes of violet-tinted lava. And in clear weather snow-capped peaks are visible to the north-east.

The plane makes for Stanleyville to the north-west, and then suddenly, without transition, the vast equatorial forest stretches away uninterruptedly to the Congo like a great ocean of trees 300 miles wide. To the traveller it is impenetrable, mysterious and inhospitable — and for a plane in difficulties most certainly fatal, for where in that vast shapeless sea of foliage could it find a safe landing place? At Stanleyville in the Congo, just below the Stanley Falls, it is another world, the world of equatorial Africa. The river, carrying along a vast volume of water, is already much larger than any of our European rivers. It flows between steep and sombre mountains overhung with luxuriant and bushy vegetation. From the fishing villages along its banks canoes made from the hollowed trunks of trees put out propelled by naked paddlers standing upright in them. There is much rain in these parts, but it falls irregularly and unpredictably, fantastically one might say. After a storm with lashing rain the blue sky reappears, incredibly blue, but invariably charged with splendid cumulus; glorious, and if I may say so, voluptuous, billowing masses of vapour. They are one of the recognized beauties of the sky, numerous almost too rich in colour, substance and density.

The equator has already been passed — it lies twenty-five miles to the south of Stanleyville. The Southern Cross is still visible in the night sky, but the Great Bear, the familiar companion of our northern nights, has reappeared, and the European has almost the impression of having already returned to his own climes. Taking off again towards the north we fly over the forest, then over plains again, and soon — for the distance is not great — at Juba the Nile appears. Flowing between its flat banks in bare and semi-desert country, it is still narrow here and the colour of coffee laced with milk and tinged with violet. Beyond Bahr el Gazal, marshland with the tints of corruption through which flows a dark infernal stream, the famous river enters the desert. Another world begins here. It is immediately recognizable as the Sahara, which, whether we will or no, is to some extent ours. It is also the Arab world, the world of Islam triumphant, contrasting with the Negro and the dark-ness of fetishism. It is another side of Africa, because the difference between the pure native of the south and the Islamized native of the north is fundamental, the former is childlike, care-free and gay, dancing and gesticulating freely, the latter is impassive and distant like an aristocrat, even oriental.

Landing from the sky at Khartoum is almost like entering a furnace. The Congo is hot, but the Nile here is burning. Sand surrounds it on both sides, and sand dust raised by the wind hangs in the air making the atmosphere heavy and tarnishing even the rays of a sun about to disappear in the dry haze of the west. What a contrast with the River Congo, always shaded with brown and green reflections and constantly enriched by the offerings of new tributaries! The Nile goes on its way alone. After the White Nile is joined by the Blue Nile at Khartoum, it receives no reinforcement whatever and yet its formidable mass of water seems to lose nothing. You find it again in Egypt, over 1200 miles further on, just as it was before, always the same, having traced its winding course through utter desert.

In following its royal valley towards Cairo past Aswan and Luxor one can measure both its infinite grandeur and its extraordinary narrowness. To right and left is the desert from which the river seems to have drained all colour by an intermediary zone of green. At certain spots inundations extend the culti-vated area which spreads out over the surrounding aridity like a sort of colonization. And then the desert returns to its basic colour, sometimes ochreous, some-times chocolate brown, whilst here and there rocky spines, black or violet, jut out of the ground as though the elementary archaean structure of the continent, the oldest of all, were thrusting its way through.

At last the Pyramids! Three small sombre triangles in the distance. And when the Delta spreads out to form a sort of Lombardy, endlessly flat and sombre, and densely populated, with innumerable villages, one realizes the aptness of the observation of Herodo-tus that Egypt is the gift of the Nile.

Africa ends at the Delta. Perhaps even Alexandria, already Mediterranean, no longer belongs to it. Let us retrace our steps. Each of those regions through which we have successively passed recalls to our mind the work of great Europeans: in South Africa and Rhodesia it was Cecil Rhodes; in Tanganyika it was Livingstone; in the Congo Stanley; at Fashoda our own Marchand; at Khartoum Gordon and Kitchener. And no doubt the names of certain great native chiefs are still alive in the memory of man: Chaka the Zulu

Napoleon, Lobengula the chief of the Matabele, Msiri at Katanga, and not forgetting the Mahdi at Omdurman. Nevertheless those great African spaces remain fundamentally anonymous, and it is one of the disturbing charms of this continent that man is lost there in a monotonous landscape which repeats itself indefinitely.

From Cairo the plane departs for Athens, Italy and Western Europe. How narrow the blue Mediterranean seems! And there is Greece, the mother of us all. The sight of that rocky soil, arid but essentially harmonious and civilized, whose headlands jut out into the sea, developed for thousands of years by a people who early arrived at maturity, illuminates in a flash for me the fundamental contrast between Africa and Mediterranean Europe, which is, after all, the most authentic Europe. On its Hellenic shores all is measure, harmony and individuality. Nature herself is civilized there, and everywhere subject to man, who has populated her thickly with his kind and made her his own.

In Greece there is not a stretch five miles long without its village, and in the evening over Italy, already in darkness, lights spring up everywhere. There is no need for a map: those capes, those straits and those gulfs have a personality of their own, one born of history as much as of geography, which permits us to identify them at once.

Africa on the other hand, seen now from afar and as though as a whole, appears massive geographically, elementary geologically, rarely suggestive of diversity, perpetually uniform and anonymous. Man is lost in an infinite immensity: measure — that sense of pro-

portion which is the source of our Western spirit —
never allows the individual to find his place, to become
conscious of a harmony between himself and the world
around him. It is that perhaps which represents the
charm of Africa for those who love to lose themselves
in something greater than themselves. It seems right
and proper that our civilization should have been
born in Greece. It seems equally right and proper
that it should not have been born in the immensity
of that dark continent, even in Egypt, which, seen
from the Parthenon, appears almost neolithic despite
her incomparable achievements. All in all, I do not
know whether the general impression I retain is that of
the endless age of African nature or the psychological
infantility of the humanity which so sparsely inhabits
it. But I do know that the great commonplace, endlessly repeated, of 'the Greek Miracle' came to me
again like a flash of truth when I glimpsed Cape
Sounioun and the Acropolis.

# CHAPTER XXV

# THE ROLE OF WHITE CIVILIZATION

'CIVIS Romanus Sum,' said Saint Paul. In the years 1898 to 1900 I made a tour of the world, and all doors opened to me when I said: 'I am a European of the white race.' And indeed, I should have been very much astonished had it not been so, because my conviction of Western supremacy was absolute. It goes without saying, I thought, and, incidentally, nothing happened to disillusion me. Looking back it would seem now that the end of the nineteenth century marked the zenith of our power in the world. The Jubilee of Queen Victoria in 1897 and Kipling's famous 'Recessional' were the symbols of an inordinate glory and pride which was to know no morrow. 'The last and most beautiful refulgence of a sun soon to fade,' wrote Barrès. When I think of it today, fifty years later, it summons up all the glory of a time now past.

Let us recall the stages of our decline. In 1904-05 Japan, an Asiatic power, was victorious over Russia. It was Europe's first defeat. And then that same Europe, divided against itself, exhausted its strength and dissipated its substance in a first and then a second terrible war which shook its prestige throughout the world. In China the Western powers lost their 'concessions'. There was even a European power to be found prepared to associate itself with Japan in an undertaking which, had it been successful, would have meant the loss of Australasia to the white race. And today another power, at least partially European, repudiates Western solidarity and strives surreptitiously to undermine the positions of the West everywhere. The French Empire in Indo-China, and the Dutch Empire in Indonesia have been shaken, whilst Britain is losing India, Ceylon and Burma. In South and Central America, countries which were regarded yesterday as belonging to the white race, such as Mexico and Bolivia, are slipping out of its grasp.

Thus in the space of half a century there has been a retreat from the furthermost edge of Western civilization. Hongkong, Singapore and Saigon are now merely far-off and threatened outposts. Australia still upholds the integrity of her 8,000,000 Whites in a continent as big as Europe by an immigration law as hermetic as she can make it, but that barrier would be swept away by an Asiatic flood if the British (or U.S.) fleet were not there to sustain the frail breastwork. The eastern coast of Africa is invaded by Indians, and Natal would not be able to defend herself for long against the flood tide if the power of Great Britain were not behind her. The pressure is ethnic; the defence is merely political. In the words of an American author, the rising tide of colour is beating against frontiers which only last century we believed, thanks to our naive confidence in our destiny, were ours for all time.

The twentieth century knows no such optimism. Disabled Europe doubts herself. The remote colonies of the white race, small garrisons surrounded and menaced by millions of coloured or yellow people, are anxiously wondering whether in the long run they will be able to maintain themselves. One hesitates to imagine what the future will be like in a hundred, even in fifty years time. And yet after all there is some reason to find that pessimism surprising. Did not the white race win a victory in the second world war as great as any it has ever known? Did it not completely destroy the only Asiatic power at all in a position to threaten it? And is it not true that everywhere else the coloured people show themselves incapable of setting up a fighting State capable of competing with the conquerors?

That is all true, and yet the white race has ceased to make progress. At a number of points it is territorially in retreat. Although China, brilliant in talents but politically anarchic, seems at the moment incapable of organizing herself as a State, the Chinese are conquering the Far East commercially. India, on the other hand, has just succeeded in obtaining her political independence. What is the future of her 400,000,000 people, prolific and invasive and the shrewdest of traders? Will they not infiltrate into all the countries bordering on the great ocean which bears their name?

We are certainly superior in organizational abilities, in that aptitude for administration on the grand scale without which there can be no industrial efficiency. Our science, and our technique founded on our science, are irresistible. Yet when the competition is no longer strictly industrial, but commercial, social and ethnic then our superiority over the East no longer looks so assured. I was disquieted, for instance, to discover in Africa that the new settlers flooding into the country from Europe no longer possessed the moral qualities which made the American pioneers successful. The twentieth-century Englishman has lost the taste for hard work. He is greatly attached to his golf and his polo, and he closes his office long before sunset and long before the end of the week. He is exigent in the matter of living standards and he despises the frugal Mediterranean — the link between the white race and the East — who is not afraid to bend his back and use his muscles to develop the soil. The Greek of Rhodes, a shrewd trader; the Syrian with his stock-in-trade upon his back; and the invasive Indian, followed by his whole family, are capturing trade both by the intensity they bring to it and by the unbelievable modesty of their personal requirements. The real 'survival of the fittest' here is the capacity to live and to survive at the least cost. We, and in particular the Anglo-Saxons, are an expensive section of the human race. Lafcadio Hearn has summed up the conditions of the competition between West and East in a terrible phrase: 'Asia can under-live Europe.' Thus, at least in the outlying regions of our empire, we are being undermined, defeated in detail and gradually replaced: the Chinese are regaining the Far East and the Indians are pacifically invading East Africa.

And yet we could easily maintain our ascendancy particularly over the coloured peoples, who are still so undeveloped, if we were not divided against ourselves and if, above all, we had not begun at the bottom of our hearts to doubt the validity of our rights. On the distant frontiers of our Western Dominion an elementary, perhaps even brutal, defensive movement is spontaneously arising. Ask an Australian, a South

African, a man from the Southern States what they mean by 'White Australia', 'White South Africa' and 'White America', and you will find that it is an unshakable and indisputable dogma for them, a passionate affirmation which brooks of not the slightest abatement. We who live so far away from the frontiers of the white race must now try to understand it, because it is a question of life and death for them. Yet we do not support them in their struggle. The Soviet Union fights against the West wherever it thinks an effective blow can be struck. And what is more paradoxical, the United States, brutally intransigent in ethnical matters at home, has done everything possible, at least she did under President Roosevelt, to break the power of the French in Indo-China, the power of the Dutch in Indonesia and the power of the British in India. Anti-colonial demagogy seems to have been at the bottom of American policy. And in our own colonial policy have we not also acted only too often according to the famous phrase: 'Let the colonies perish rather than a principle!' And in the United Nations Organization, the creation of Western civilization, the votes of the white race are probably not the majority.

From all that has gone before I must conclude that though the West may be threatened from without it is even more threatened from within. Now without being a racial fanatic I must insist that it is upon the white race, and on it alone, that the responsibility for Western civilization rests: if that race is endangered, or should it disappear, then inevitably that civilization will be endangered or will disappear with it. How should it defend itself? Western civilization as we conceive it is a collection of techniques supported and maintained by a collection of values. To turn to technique alone would be to betray our culture, but to follow the logic of our principles without restraint would be equivalent to suicide.

Expanding and conquering for so long, the West now gives the impression of being on the defensive. When I was in India and China at the turn of the century I had no such impression. Our hegemony seemed assured. But since 1918 I have been conscious of the precarious nature of our hold on Australia. Since the second world war I have realized something that I was never taught at school, namely that South America does not belong indisputably to the white race. And now I have just been forced to consider to what extent the occupation of Africa by the white race is a temporary and superficial thing with no guarantee of a future. And in considering the rhythm of world development as it has been hurried on for the past two generations it seems to me that I have witnessed a retreat of civilization comparable to that of the Roman Empire when it found itself forced to defend itself on all sides against the rising tide of barbarism which threatened to engulf it. I can no longer say everywhere with the pride of former days: CIVIS ROMANUS SUM.